Niche Dominance® F
The following are Niche Dominance b‌u‌o‌.‌.‌

"*Niche Dominance is an easy read for business owners who want a clearer understanding of digital marketing services and a strategy for achieving online success. I recommend that you buy this book before your competitors do!*"

-Dr. Joe Vitale, author of *The Attractor Factor* and *The Key* and featured in the movie *The Secret*

"*A must read for business owners, entrepreneurs, and internet marketing consultants worldwide, Niche Dominance demystifies digital marketing for small businesses in a clear, easy-to-understand manner. Whether you're new to marketing online or simply want to improve your strategy, this book offers the ultimate structure for incorporating a highly effective internet marketing plan.*"

-Ivan Misner, Ph.D., NY Times Bestselling Author and Founder of BNI®

"*Outsourcing digital marketing services is a big decision for any business, and it's imperative that you choose the right provider the first time around. Niche Dominance will help you understand what's involved in marketing your business online and how to ask the right questions to ensure you hire the right provider the first time around. Highly recommended!*"

- Stephanie Chandler, author of *Own Your Niche* & founder of Authority Publishing

NICHE DOMINANCE™

NICHE DOMINANCE™

CREATING ORDER OUT OF YOUR DIGITAL MARKETING CHAOS

JOHN S. RIZZO & V. MICHAEL SANTORO

Published by
Globe On-Demand, LLC
877-609-6762
www.GlobeOnDemand.com

Table of Contents

Acknowledgements

As with anything of the magnitude of this undertaking, it is never done alone, and it would never have happened without the input from our valued clients, Internet marketing colleagues and networking associates.

Our networking groups include:

The Charleston Metro Chamber of Commerce
(http://www.CharlestonChamber.net)

Business Networking International (BNI)
(http://www.bni.com)

Service Corps of Retired Executives (SCORE)
(http://score.org)

Network for Teaching Entrepreneurship (NFTE)
(http://nfte.com)

Additionally, we also appreciate the manuscript feedback and encouragement provided by Christine Rizzo and Joseph Rizzo. Lastly, we are indebted to Laurie Sharp, our editor, for the countless hours that turned our manuscript into a professional book, as well as Julie Csizmadia for her outstanding job with designing our book's cover and interior design.

We also thank you for taking the time to read our book. We hope that it helps you to achieve added business success.

Introduction

Globe On-Demand, LLC is an Internet technology company dedicated to helping our clients achieve Niche Dominance™ through effective digital marketing and branding campaigns. We developed this strategy after a two-year process of interviewing over 100 small and local businesses, as well as entrepreneurs, through networking groups and testing various technologies with our clients. We also analyzed the rapidly changing online environment and consumer user behavior that is impacting businesses. The following are our findings:

USER BEHAVIOR IS CHANGING

Consumers are increasingly using technology to influence their buying decisions. This includes seeking out the best deals and reading reviews, as well as finding relevant and convenient solutions to their problems.

Even when consumers see a traditional advertisement, they use the Internet for more information. Increasingly, they are using their mobile devices to search and contact local businesses. Their search behavior while using their mobile devices is also different.

COMPUTER USAGE

Currently consumers use their computers as a research tool to locate additional information about products, services and companies. They also conduct price comparisons prior to making a purchase.

MOBILE DEVICE USAGE

They use their mobile devices to take immediate action including finding directions, obtaining contact information and utilizing popular social media platforms. Additionally, there is an increasing trend of making purchases using mobile devices.

CHANGING CUSTOMER EXPECTATIONS

Customers expect businesses to convince them they are serious about helping and not just trying to take their money. The benefits offered, including an ongoing commitment, are of paramount importance to them. It is this message communicated through technology that is necessary to attract and keep new customers. In this day of social media, they are motivated to share their experiences and do so regularly. Help them and they will remain loyal; disappoint them and not only will you lose them, they may destroy your reputation by posting highly visible bad reviews. Unlike unfavorable traditional press fading away with time, a bad online review can last indefinitely.

THE CHANGING DIGITAL LANDSCAPE

As this consumer behavior is analyzed by the major search engine and social media companies such as Google and Facebook, they are rapidly updating their technologies to better serve their users. They are also fiercely competing to gain an advantage and continually adding new features in order to retain and gain market share. Furthermore, companies such as Facebook and Bing are in strategic alliances to accelerate growth. These changes are dramatically impacting the digital landscape. This is causing chaos, as well as overwhelming both internet marketing service providers and businesses. Difficulty understanding how to implement these changes into a sustainable digital marketing plan is impacting online success.

INTERNET MARKETING SERVICE PROVIDERS

The Internet marketing arena is viewed as a carnival, with businesses receiving calls daily pitching them to "step right up" and buy a variety of shiny objects - all offering a Page One ranking.

While there are many good companies, currently there are no standards required for individuals or businesses to offer digital marketing services. Unfortunately, all it takes is a professional website to join the online marketing frenzy. Additionally, even an inexperienced person can sound knowledgeable by becoming fluent in the buzz words. Many digital marketing courses being sold today encourage people to get a local business client first and then figure out how to deliver the services. These vendors are either not qualified or behind on the rapid technological changes that are required to produce online marketing results.

To compound the situation, many digital service vendors offer only part of the necessary solution for a business to achieve a competitive advantage. Even when they outsource or partner to offer additional services, the implementation is disjointed and does not follow a plan. Some are even unwilling to work with other companies and only offer what they can provide.

Working with multiple vendors offering different services such as SEO, pay-per-click advertising or social media can actually hurt a business' bottom line because of poor implementation. The poor overall results occurred when the components lacked continuity rather than operating from a cohesive plan.

BUSINESS OWNERS

Our findings indicated that business owners have migrated from questioning the validity of digital marketing to knowing that it is now a requirement. However, most business owners did not understand what online marketing involves, and viewed it as simply a Page One ranking for their website. They found digital marketing to be abstract and confusing because they could not relate it to traditional, more tangible advertising methods such as Yellow Page listings. Most had a bad experience with online marketing vendors and viewed services like SEO as a scam. This generated a major concern about trusting digital marketing vendors, causing procrastination and stress about choosing the right resource.

Rather than do it themselves, these frustrated business owners unanimously desired to outsource to a trusted vendor who could create a marketing plan to produce short term results while building a long term foundation.

THE NICHE DOMINANCE SOLUTION

Our solution to these issues is helping our clients take a Niche Dominance approach to gain a competitive advantage. We've invested two years developing Niche Dominance to meet these needs, testing every major component of digital marketing and developing an integrated solution that delivers on these objectives for our clients.

It is both a business mindset and an integrated process. The mission is to develop a commanding digital presence to brand our clients as an authority, while increasing their bottom line through planned online marketing activity. The objective is to utilize technology to communicate effectively with potential customers. With Niche Dominance, businesses don't sell; they allow potential customers to buy.

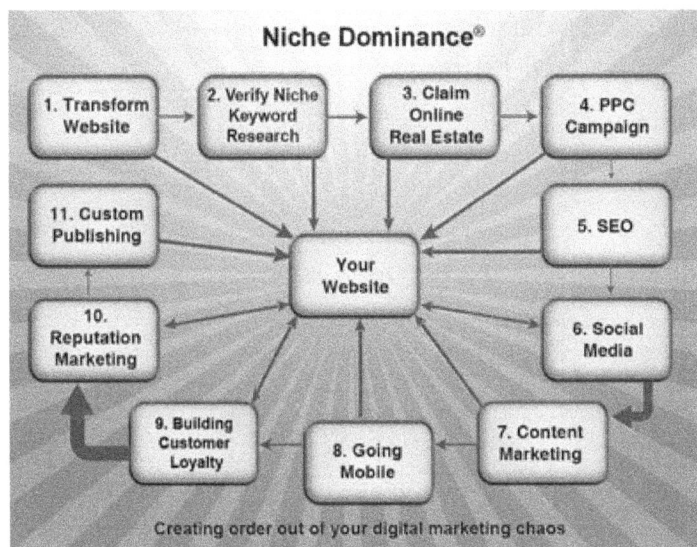

Niche Dominance®

1. Transform Website

2. Verify Niche Keyword Research

3. Claim Online Real Estate

4. PPC Campaign

11. Custom Publishing

5. SEO

Your Website

10. Reputation Marketing

6. Social Media

9. Building Customer Loyalty

8. Going Mobile

7. Content Marketing

Creating order out of your digital marketing chaos

After reading Niche Dominance you will have a better understanding of what digital marketing services are, how they work, and how they need to be correctly implemented to achieve maximum results. We also provide the questions to ask vendors to ensure you are hiring the best resources. This is helpful if you wish to manage the process yourself instead of hiring an Internet marketing consulting firm to oversee management.

It is time to transition to a competitive mindset and use it to outsmart the competition. With Niche Dominance, the focus will no longer be on the competition but rather on properly servicing new customers.

Wishing every business owner great success,
John S. Rizzo and V. Michael Santoro

For complete information, please visit us at:
http://www.NicheDominance.com

{ CHAPTER 1 }

A Tour of Google Page One

While the major search engines work similarly, we are using Google in our example as it commands 66.2% of the core search share according to comScore.

Achieving a Page One placement in the major search engines is a great accomplishment considering the fierce competition. However, most business owners do not understand what this means to their business, nor the different ways it can be achieved. Most think ranking for their business name is all they need to be successful. Unfortunately, this is a false sense of accomplishment that can actually be costing you money.

Google and the other major search engines are primarily "keyword-driven" in order to return their search results. The returned results will differ based upon the search being national or local. When a surfer types in their topic of interest, Google returns results for that topic. For example, if you typed in *dentist in Hartford*, Google will display the advertisements, Google+ Local listings and the top organic results associated with the *dentist in Hartford* search phrase. Additionally, if the keyword phrase is entered without the location, e.g. dentist, then Google checks the location (computer's IP address) to determine the surfer's location and will display the appropriate PPC ads and Google+ Local listings. If the search does not have local intent, then the Google+ Local listing may not display.

Increasingly Google is showing users signed in to Gmail, Google+, and other Google products personalized results based on history and connectivity to what others in their network shared. The rest of the displayed results will depend on how well the websites are optimized to serve the users. For instance, a directory site that offers help to locate a dentist can rank on Page One even though it is not local.

FIVE WAYS TO ACHIEVE A PAGE ONE PLACEMENT

The Five Ways to Achieve a Page One placement are as follows:

- Search engine marketing, also known as pay-per-click advertising

- Google+ Local, as well as Bing and Yahoo local listing

- Organic search listing for your web pages (referred to as the "top 10") ranking because of relevance to the search terms, as opposed to their being advertisements

- Organic search listing for your video, article, press release, social media profiles/posts and other marketing material

- Organic search listing for a major directory site, such as Yelp

Each of these topics are covered in detail in other chapters. However, it is important to understand the structure behind a Page One listing and what it means to your business.

SEARCH ENGINE MARKETING (SEM)

With SEM, which is also called pay-per-click (PPC) advertising, ads display both at the top and right side of the search results, as well as within specific products, such as Gmail. This is paid advertising and does not require any search engine optimization or waiting months to see results. The following are the benefits and challenges:

Benefits

- Ads can be displayed in a few hours or less and target both Internet and mobile network users.

- SEM produces quality, targeted traffic based upon the keywords you bid on.

- These SEM ad campaigns determine "money" keyword phrases that produce sales and can be used for your website's SEO to generate free organic Page One buyer traffic.

Challenges

- SEM can be expensive and for some niches cost prohibitive.

- If a PPC campaign is not managed properly, your business can lose money very quickly.

- If the advertising stops, the traffic stops and you immediately lose your Page One placement.

- SEM only produces about 2.5% of the total Page One traffic available for the keyword phrase. That is actually only about two visitors for every 100 surfers.

- PPC traffic from mobile devices may not convert if landing pages are not mobile friendly.

GOOGLE+ LOCAL LISTING

Benefits

- A Google+ Local listing is free and displays prominently on Page One for both computer and mobile users.

- This listing customizes information to your business, including images and videos. Google has even developed a service to actually take pictures of the inside of your business.

- Customers can add testimonials to give your business credibility.

- Customers can offer exclusive Google+ Local deals.

Challenges

- Ranking on Page One for your Google+ Local listing can be very competitive.

- Google+ Local ranking can be impacted if inconsistent business information is found on other online properties such as your website and business directories.

- You need a physical business address and unique phone number for the specific location in order to rank.

- There must be on-going activity like testimonials and citations to achieve and maintain a top ranking, or your ranking can fall to Page Two or lower.

- Your Google+ Local listing could be sabotaged by competitors if left unclaimed.

- Google can arbitrarily gather inaccurate business details about your business that can be merged with your Google+ Local listing.

SEARCH ENGINE OPTIMIZATION (SEO) ORGANIC SEARCH

Benefits

- It provides a source of continuous free traffic.

- SEO produces the most traffic available on Page One.

- You can rank for individual web pages and not just your home page.

- You can also rank on Page One for several keyword phrases.

- SEO rankings can continue long term with a sound SEO program.

Challenges

- It can often take four to six months to achieve a Page One ranking.

- A Top Five ranking is necessary to produce the most traffic.

- Ranking results are volatile and achieving a Page One ranking may not be permanent.

- Retaining rankings requires a monthly ongoing SEO campaign.

- A Page Two or lower ranking will produce little, if any, traffic.

- SEO traffic from mobile devices may not convert if website is not mobile friendly.

Social Media

Social media marketing refers to the process of gaining website traffic or attention through social media sites including Facebook, GooglePlus, Twitter, LinkedIn and YouTube. Most offer the option for both a personal and a business page. The personal profile can be used for personal branding while the business page can be used for customer service or reputation management.

NOTE: As the GooglePlus page can influence your website rankings, you want to make it part of your SEO campaign as well. Discuss this with your Internet marketing consultant as Google continues to evolve this service.

Benefits

- Brand your business as an authority and increase trust online.

- This is an easy way to connect with customers in real time.

- Social media increases ways to build relationships with customers.

- Your SEO rankings can be improved if social media is used correctly.

- B2B connections that are otherwise difficult to obtain with traditional networking can be improved with social media.

- Your excellent social media content can go viral and help build more loyal followers.

- Social media sites are mobile friendly to support the majority of traffic.

Challenges

- Long term strategy may not produce immediate revenue.

- Social media is very labor intensive and can prove to be expensive.

- The strategy needs to be developed, as simple arbitrary postings will not produce desirable results.

Content Marketing

Content marketing refers to publishing content for online directories and Web 2.0 properties to share with others. Uploading a video about your business to YouTube with links back to your website is one example of content marketing. You can also publish articles and audio podcasts, as well as build free Web 2.0 properties, that link back to your website. Web 2.0 properties allow you to post and share content about your business or topics of interest. Since sales pitches are frowned upon, good content can brand you as an authority online. Examples of these sites are Squidoo.com, HubPages.com and WetPaint.com.

Benefits

- Marketing material can help achieve a Page One placement.

- Good content can brand your business as an authority online.

- Links from your posted content benefits your website's SEO rankings.

- Google loves video and Web 2.0 properties, and can rank them quickly.

- The content directories and Web 2.0 properties such as YouTube, ITunes, EzineArticles, Squidoo and Hubpages also generate traffic to your website.

- Your content can go viral if people decide its value is worth sharing.

Challenges

- Creating original quality content is a challenge for most business owners.

- Google can penalize duplicate content, which means distributing the same material to multiple directories and Web 2.0 properties.

- Uploaded content may not rank and will be buried from view if not optimized properly.

- Professional content marketing material like video creation requires an investment of time and money.

WHAT A PAGE ONE PLACEMENT MEANS TO YOUR BUSINESS

A Page One ranking is all about generating targeted traffic by achieving and maintaining a Top Five position. This is becoming more difficult as more businesses are competing for top placement. Imagine thousands of websites all vying for a Page One placement.

The following table demonstrates the importance of striving for better organic search engine ranking:

Google Position	% Clicks	Traffic per 1,000	Traffic Increase by Position
1	36.4	364	From 2 to 1: 191%
2	12.5	125	From 3 to 2: 32%
3	9.5	95	From 4 to 3: 20%
4	7.9	79	From 5 to 4: 30%
5	6.1	61	From 6 to 5: 49%
6	4.1	41	
7	3.8	38	

The table above is based upon 1,000 searches and how the traffic is divided among the Top Seven organic rankings. If your web page has a Number One placement, it can receive

36.4% of the traffic. If you currently have a Number Two listing and then achieve a Number One listing, your traffic can increase by 191%!

NOTE: This table does not include the traffic resulting from the PPC ads displayed at the top and right side of the page. PPC ads generate about 2.5% of the available traffic.

{ CHAPTER 2 }

How the Internet Works for your Business

The goal of a sound Internet marketing plan can be divided into two components: targeted traffic and conversions. There are specific requirements necessary to achieve success with both components.

TARGETED TRAFFIC

Targeted traffic, whether local or national, is achieved when your web pages and digital marketing material is found by surfers interested in finding a business like yours. When they click on your link in the search results or on one of your ads and visit your web page, this is considered traffic to your website. For this traffic to be valuable, it must be targeted. For example, if you are a personal injury lawyer located in Charleston and people in Tampa are visiting your site, you will probably not acquire many new clients. Conversely, if someone in Chicago with lower back pain is searching for a remedy using the keyword phrase, "how to get rid of lower back pain" and they visit your E-Commerce site, there is a good chance that you will make a product sale, even if you are located in California.

WEBSITE CONVERSIONS

Having targeted traffic visiting a website that offers confusing content with no call to action reduces the chance of obtaining new customers. It can also hurt your search engine rankings. A website conversion is having your targeted traffic take action when they visit your website. Examples of a call to action include:

- Calling your company for a specific reason.

- Filling out a form for more information or to receive a discount coupon.

- Scheduling a free consultation.

- Having an online chat to answer a specific question, or

- Making a purchase.

YOU HAVE ONLY SEVEN SECONDS OR YOUR VISITORS ARE GONE!

Unfortunately, many business websites are no more than a billboard and potential customers are confused as to what to do. This may cause them to leave in frustration and move on to a competitor's site. You have seven seconds to get a visitor to take action or they're gone, *and that's a proven statistic.* Having a website that provides original quality content and a clear call to action dramatically increases your chances of converting your traffic into customers.

For instance, one of our new clients expressed concern that they were not receiving the expected amount of consultations.

After reviewing the traffic statistics, the conversions were proportionately low for the amount of traffic. Upon reviewing their website, we discovered that it took three clicks for a potential patient to locate the form to schedule a consultation. Also, the phone number was not prominently placed on the pages. We restructured the site and added the consultation sign up form and phone number to every web page. This reduced the amount of clicks and navigation required to schedule a consultation. The result was that the amount of consultations tripled. We then worked to increase the traffic which further increased the amount of consultations.

{ CHAPTER 3 }

How do the Search Engines Work?

To rank in the search engines requires a two-step process. The first step is indexing your web pages into their database. This is how they keep track of your website's existence and store the associated information. The second process is assigning a ranking to your site. The search engines use software called *spiders*. The spiders patrol the Internet, reporting back information about websites. The search engines evaluate the data and assign each web page a position. For example, a new site initially may not rank in the top 1000 results.

When the search engines evaluate your site, they initially look at the site's subject, e.g. dieting, plumbing, etc. They then evaluate the content, record the website's links and document the number of pages. This is not a one-time only process. The spiders visit sites on a regular basis to evaluate and document the changes. Many times, if the page navigation is confusing, the spiders can miss some of the web pages and they will not be indexed. An important aspect is that each website page is associated with keyword phrases, and that is why each page should be optimized for different keyword phrases and rank on its own. The search engines can actually rank one of your pages higher than another.

BUILDING YOUR WEBSITE'S AUTHORITY

The most critical part for any website is building your website's authority in the eyes of the search engines. The more important your website is viewed, the higher your web pages will rank. Google determines your website's value by how well your web pages are optimized and the number of one-way back links pointing to your site. The rationale is that if another site links to you without you linking back, called a one-way back link, then your website must be providing valuable content.

Once they analyze your website, Google assigns your site a page rank (PR) from 0 to 10. Most new sites are a PR 0 until they have some time to age and generate back links. It is a complex evolving algorithm, which changed over 600 times in 2011. However, to convey the concept, each PR number is exponentially higher than the preceding number. For example, a PR 1 site is viewed 10 times more important than a PR 0. A PR 2 ranking is 10 times more important than a PR 1, and so on. It requires a well-optimized website with both excellent original content and adding one-way back links continuously over time to increase your site's page rank (PR).

Google likes natural growth and will penalize websites that try to game the system. For example, adding 1,000 back links today and then stopping is considered spamming the search engines and your site could be banned. With Google, the tortoise wins the ranking race. Your website's PR will increase over time if you slowly and continuously add back links, as well as quality well-optimized content. Additionally, this adds to a better user experience.

Remember, PR can fluctuate based upon your website's activity. If you stop adding back links or allow your website to remain stagnant, your PR value can drop. Your hard-earned page placement can also drop. Additionally, Google is hiring human reviewers to check top ranking sites to ensure quality. If a low quality site is ranking and a human reviewer catches it, the site will definitely be dropped from Page One.

UNDERSTANDING THE GOOGLE DANCE

Every business wants immediate results for their investment and it is no different with Internet marketing. If you are in a hurry for results, then run a PPC campaign while you are waiting for your web pages to rank organically on Page One. You cannot rush SEO and trying to do so will hurt your rankings. What will drive you crazy is what is referred to as the "Google Dance!" When your site is indexed and initially ranked, you will notice that your website will be nowhere to be found. Then suddenly, it may appear on Page Three; in a day or so, you might see it on Page One! You jump for joy, only to see it disappear once again into the search engine abyss. Eventually, the Google Dance stops and your site will settle down; that is considered the bench mark to begin measuring future progress. This is natural as Google evaluates the site and works to establish a ranking…it is not your Internet marketing consultant!

CONCLUSION

Make sure you work with a reputable Internet marketing resource who thoroughly understands search engine optimization (SEO). No one can guarantee your SEO results since Google and the other search engines make the rules. Additionally, be wary of vendors who call PPC advertising SEO. Many vendors guarantee a Page One placement by calling it SEO and then use PPC for generating traffic. Remember, if the advertising stops, so does the traffic and your web pages will not have any ranking. You need a good SEO program to get your web pages ranked for the long term. SEO can produce long term, free traffic with a top Page One position.

NICHE DOMINANCE

Niche Dominance is comprised of 11 digital orders of business that when implemented correctly, offer a competitive advantage. In the following chapters we will outline these 11 digital orders of business in detail. It is imperative that they be implemented according to a plan to produce the best results.

{ CHAPTER 4 }

Digital Order of Business #1: Transforming your Website into a Business Asset

An Internet marketing consultant will begin with an in-depth review of your current online presence. Think of this as an audit of your current environment. This helps to determine what is working, missing or not working. It also includes a competitive analysis for how you are ranking compared to your competition. The result of this audit will be the benchmark for the project; and will determine the plan for establishing your online infrastructure. The first step is to compile your business information that will be used to help your resource claim your online properties. See Appendix A for checklist. The next steps are to ensure that your website conveys your unique selling proposition, the benefits you provide and your site's ability to convert traffic into customers.

Your company website is not a "nice to have" part of your business; it needs to become an essential business tool. To build your online presence, you need to transform your website into a business asset. When your website begins to generate new business on autopilot, and you can measure your return on investment (ROI) that adds to the overall value of your business.

This chapter will discuss the various components of your website, as well as the alternatives available if you need one developed. However, first compile your business information as your digital marketing resources will need access to your website, blog and online real estate. This is required to update your site, create a Google+ Local listing, and make your content search engine friendly. See Appendix A for a checklist.

DOMAIN NAME (URL)

Your domain name or URL is the most essential part of your online presence. It is the asset that *you need to own.* Many businesses have their web designer register their domain name when their website is being built. Realize that if this is the case, then your web designer owns the domain name and NOT you. We recommend that you check to verify that you own your domain and if not, have it transferred into your name. We have heard horror stories from business owners about being held hostage over their domain name.

Imagine if you decide to change web designers and they get angry about losing the business and decide to keep your company's domain name. They have the right to shut down your site or even sell the domain name! This is a worst case scenario, but it is good practice to deal with this proactively, and not from a point of weakness if the relationship sours.

If you did not personally register and pay for your domain name or are not sure if it is registered in your name, complete the following:

- Go to http://www.GoDaddy.com.

- Enter your domain name into the search box and click the "Go" button.

- Next to the message that states that your domain name is already taken is a link, *Get info*. Click on it.

- Scroll down and see if you are listed under "Registrant." This is the owner of the domain name. If it is not listed as either you or your business, then you need to have it transferred.

DOMAIN NAME OWNERSHIP TRANSFER

To obtain ownership of your domain name, do the following:

- Call your web designer or current owner of the domain and indicate that you would prefer to have it registered to your business, as it is standard practice.

- Contact the domain name registrar where the domain was registered; advise them that you wish to set up an account and that a domain name will be transferred to the account. If the registrar is difficult to contact or does not respond, you can call GoDaddy and they will set up a free account for you over the phone. They will also instruct you through the process required to transfer the domain.

- When your web designer responds to the transfer verification process, you will become the new owner and be billed the renewal fee annually. You can also register the domain name for multiple years or have it automatically renew when the registration payment is due.

CHOOSING A DOMAIN NAME

If you currently do not have a website and plan to invest in having one developed, you will need to choose and register a domain name to represent your business online. Many businesses use their name. However, a better alternative is to select a domain name that is a keyword phrase representing your business. This technique works well for SEO rankings. Your Internet marketing consultant can conduct the keyword research and explore the available domains for the keyword phrases. An example is, "Tampa Locksmith." The following is the criteria for selecting a keyword rich domain:

- The keyword phrase you choose should have monthly traffic.

- Limit the phrase to three or four words in length.

- Try to avoid using hyphens if possible, like South-Tampa-Locksmith.

- Use only a .com, .net or .org extension.

- A .mobi domain name can be used for your mobile website

NOTE: The first choice is to obtain a .com extension. If it is not available, then the other extensions will be sufficient.

There are several keyword phrases for most niches and with a little research you can find a keyword-rich domain name that will help with your SEO rankings.

TIP: If you already have a business domain name and it is being used on your business cards and/or printed marketing material, you can forward the business domain name to the keyword-rich domain name and it will be transparent to the surfer. This helps your website's SEO while preserving the investment in your business cards and printed material. This is an example:

http://www.AcmeLocksmithInc.com ▸ http://www. LocksmithInBoston.com

WEBSITE HOSTING

In order to have a website online, you need to use a web server that is attached to the Internet. Once you establish an account, your hosting provider will email you the DNS addresses associated with your website. After logging into your domain registration account such as GoDaddy, update your domain name with these addresses. This action points your domain name to your website, and usually can be performed by your web designer.

Hosting is no longer expensive; however, many vendors will charge you for items that are already included in their hosting packages. When we perform an initial review for a new client, we check the current monthly charges and have been amazed at what some vendors are charging. We discovered one vendor charging fees for domain management, bandwidth usage, and hosting in excess of $1500 per month.

Many vendors sell hosting to small and local businesses, only to buy it from the same hosting accounts that you could have bought from directly. However, it is fair to pay your vendor for technical support if you wish assistance with any issues that may arise.

As with your domain name, we suggest that you own your hosting account. Once you sign up, your web designer can then upload your website files. This allows you to change web designers and Internet marketing vendors without impacting your website or interrupting your business.

TIP: Remember it is good practice to change the passwords for your hosting and domain registration accounts when you change vendors.

CHANGING HOSTING PROVIDERS

If you decide to own your own hosting account, you will have to move your current website to the new hosting service and change your domain name's DNS addresses as described above. We provide this service for our clients and your Internet marketing resource can do so as well. You will need FTP (user name and password) access to your current hosting account; this is necessary to log in and download your current website. If you do not have this information, you need to obtain it from your current hosting provider.

Ensure that your resource understands how to move a website or you can run into issues when your new hosting account is cut over. For instance, your email may not work unless the new accounts are set up on the new hosting account. The following is an itemized list of what may be an issue:

- Email accounts, including remote access by handheld devices,

- Any scripts or software functionality that requires a database, including shopping carts, web based applications and customer log in functionality, and

- SSL security certificates.

Most local or small business sites are comprised of simple HTML files and are easy to move, nonetheless, be sure that the email accounts are created prior to cut over. If you are using a template-driven site that includes vendor content and hosting, then you may not be able to move the site. Instead, you will have to create a new website built on your own hosting account.

WEBSITE OPTIONS

If you do not have a website or are looking to have a web designer build you a new one, there are a variety of options. Because of the need to achieve top search engine rankings, you must consider SEO, as well as the amount of ongoing changes required, when you select a platform. If you make frequent changes or need to add content continuously, then paying for these changes can become pricey.

First, for a local or small business that is not selling several products online, you do not need to invest thousands of dollars into a website design. What works best is a professional looking layout with good navigation; providing your visitors with helpful content will far outweigh the "bells and whistles." The most important aspects for a well-designed website include:

- Your content

- How it is optimized for search engine ranking

- Effective calls to action to convert traffic into customers

- Keeping your content updated regularly

- Finding ways to improve user experience

NOTE: It has become important to add the social media icons that link to your social media pages, such as Facebook, LinkedIn, Twitter, Google +1 and YouTube. This allows users to share information about your business with their network and builds social proof for your website.

WEBSITE ALTERNATIVES

Standard Websites

If a web designer is going to design a new standard website for your business with static pages, discuss the options available for updating content and adding pages on a regular basis. There are content management programs that work with standard websites, but they can be expensive. Either negotiate a reasonable fee to have the changes and updates provided, or find a local resource or college student who knows how to use a web page editor. Ensure that the resource is reliable. Before beginning, have them back up the original files; if there is an error or technical issue, they can upload the original files.

Content Management Systems

Google loves blogs and ranks them well. Even if you have a standard website, we recommend that you add a WordPress blog to your site. Your web designer can use WordPress to design your primary site and you can easily log in and make changes yourself. Also, because WordPress is a popular platform, you can find reasonably priced resources to update your site.

Niche Template Sites

There are many niche specific hosting and web development companies that offer website solutions. We have seen them for lawyers, dentists, plumbers, etc, providing content in the form of articles and videos within a template layout. You have pages such as Home Page and About Us page where you can enter your own unique content by logging into a content management system. They will host the site and you can use your own domain name. It is an easy way to immediately have a website.

With the recent Google changes, duplicate content can prevent your web pages from ranking in the search engines. This can be a major issue using these options.

TIP: To see if the site contains duplicate content, go to one of their websites and copy a random sentence up to 32 words and paste into a Google search. Put the sentence in quotes, for example, "These are eight of the most amazing tips to help you with your widget." If it is original content, only that website will appear in the search results. If it is duplicate content, all the websites where the content is used will appear.

The fairest way to evaluate this type of website is to inform them of your duplicate content concern and the results that you discovered. Ask if your Internet marketing or SEO resource can edit the duplicate pages and optimize them for better SEO results.

Flash Sites

Flash sites are very appealing and can contain some really cool effects; however, a 100% Flash site is challenging for achieving good SEO rankings and is not mobile friendly. The reason for this is that the content is embedded in a flash movie file and although the site can be indexed by Google, the problem is that elements such as the site's navigation structure, is harder to index. Additionally, the site ranks for only a single URL. It is better to switch to an HTML5 format or remove the navigation from the Flash movie.

If you like Flash effects, then incorporate the movie as part of a standard web page, or use Flash as an animated header graphic along with text-based content. You get the movie effects and the search engines get to review your content.

Website Content

Content is king and Google will reward your site with great search engine placement if you provide plenty of original quality content.

What Is Quality Content?

Quality content is not determined by how well it is written editorially, but rather the way Google views how expertly it is written. It reviews your web pages and looks for the theme-based words that are included. For example, if a doctor were to write an article on heart trouble, he or she would include certain terminology, such as Cardiovascular and Cardiomyopathy. Google compares the content to a database of associated theme keywords and phrases. The more theme words that are used in well written content the higher the quality score and page ranking.

NOTE: If the keywords are not used naturally within the content and are "stuffed" into a list, the content may not rank well.

Determining Your Content

The free information that you provide for your website and online marketing material needs to be based upon your niche keyword phrases, and must offer good information about the topic. Do not recycle general or common sense material. Your free content needs to address topics and information not easily found on the web. It needs to brand you as an authority.

For example, which paragraph appears to be written by an expert?

> **Sentence 1:** "If you are experiencing *lower back pain,* you are not alone. Nearly everyone at some point in their life has back pain that interferes with work, routine daily activities or recreation."

> **Sentence 2:** "The spaces between your *vertebrae* are maintained by round, *spongy pads of cartilage* called *intervertebral discs* that allow for flexibility in the *lower back* and act

much like shock absorbers throughout the *spinal column* to cushion the *bones* as the body moves."

Which sentence do you think was written by someone with a good knowledge of the spine? Obviously, the second sentence has a better chance of ranking in the search engines even though both sentences read editorially correct.

Duplicate Content Penalties

Using the same content on multiple pages within your website should be avoided. This can trigger a duplicate content penalty which means that your web pages will not rank highly in the search engines. Just ensure that you rewrite your content so it reads differently even though it has a similar meaning.

For example: "For more information about how we can help you, visit our services description page."

Rewrite on another page: "If you desire more information about how Acme can assist you, please review our services description web page."

In addition, make sure that each page is at least 800 - 1,000 words in length. Using video to connect with your visitors is also important.

CALL TO ACTION

Even the best content may not help you obtain new customers if it does not contain a call to action. A call to action informs your visitors of what you want them to do next. For instance, you can encourage them to:

- *Call* 1-888-123-4567 Now for a free estimate

- *Fill out* the contact us form to schedule a consultation

- *Click on* the chat button to see how we can help you

- *Make* a purchase

- *Schedule* an online demo

- *Download* free white paper

- *Free trial,* no credit card required

TIP: It is important to make it easy for them to act. If you say "call now," be sure to list the phone number even though it is on your banner at the top of the page. If you ask them to fill out a form, have it available on the page. Do not make your customers have to hunt for anything.

Your digital marketing consultant can advise you how to create compelling content that includes the necessary calls to action.

MEASURING RETURN ON INVESTMENT AND TRAFFIC STATISTICS

Many businesses spend money on marketing and advertising to get new customers and mistakenly judge the success by whether their phone rings and they make sales. It is wise to evaluate whether the individual campaigns are profitable. Putting in this type of system allows you to test and subsequently keep what is working and stop what is not profitable.

The first thing to do is be sure that Google Analytics is installed on your web pages. Google Analytics is free and provides a wealth of information about your website traffic. Google Analytics provides information including:

- The keyword phrases that visitors used to find your site

- The bounce rate

- How long your visitors remained on your site

- The traffic sources

- Social media engagement

- Types of mobile devices that are accessing your site

- Visitor demographics

Google also provides free tracking numbers where available. If there are no numbers available in your area, there are low cost services that provide different tracking phone numbers. Remember, you must use a specific phone number for each marketing campaign.

For instance, if you try a banner ad campaign, using a different phone number and email address will show the activity for that campaign. All you do is log into the call tracking service and see the activity for each phone number. Many vendors include this call tracking service and web traffic statistics for your campaigns, so ask before you pay for tracking numbers.

NOTE: You can compare a vendor's statistics against your Google Analytics statistics for accuracy. Another tip is to view the keyword phrases captured by Google Analytics for each month. It will show you the keyword phrases plus the amount of traffic each one generated. When you determine the keyword phrases that are producing consistent traffic, you can then use them in your online advertising campaigns.

COUPON CODES

When advertising, you can also use coupon codes to track success. Require the visitor to enter a coupon code on your website to obtain a specific advertised discount. Assign a different code for each campaign. If you are advertising on three different sites, have a different coupon code for each and you can then see which site is generating the most sales.

NOTE: You should also use different tracking methods for each of your traditional advertising campaigns, such as bill boards, TV and radio ads, newspaper ads, etc. The majority of people who see a traditional ad will visit the business' website before calling, so it is advisable to consistently tie your code tracking between your traditional advertising and your website.

Although the technology is available, many businesses do not track their advertising campaigns to measure their return on investment. If you use an Internet marketing consultant, it is essential to discuss how he or she can consolidate your tracking and measure the ROI for each campaign. That will identify what is working so you can either keep investing or reinvest in other new things.

CHAPTER 5

Digital Order of Business #2: Verify your Niche and Validate Keyword Research

Once Digital Order of Business #1 identifies any issues and begins resolving them, your digital marketing consultant will ensure that your specific niche is verified. He or she will then conduct or validate the keyword research to target the correct audience. For example, a dentist who specialized in implants wants to target patients with missing teeth, as opposed to those looking for an orthodontist to have their kid's teeth straightened.

HOW KEYWORD PHRASES IMPACT YOUR BUSINESS

Many businesses achieve a false sense of accomplishment if they are ranking on Page One for their business name or a single keyword phrase associated with their business. If no one is searching for your business name, then ranking number one for it will not produce any results. To better understand what your potential business opportunity is from ranking on Page One, you need to determine the number of keyword phrases and total amount of monthly searches that are associated with your business. This is a more complete traffic picture.

It is imperative that you use the same keyword phrases that people are actually using to locate a business like yours. Don't guess! Guessing can result in good search engine placement for a keyword phrase that produces little or no traffic.

Digital marketing consultants use keyword research tools to locate the keyword phrases associated with a root keyword phrase. For example, typing in "dentist Tampa" will display the associated keyword phrases for this local business, how many monthly searches there are for each, as well as the estimated cost-per-click (CPC):

Keyword Phrases	Monthly Searches	Approximate CPC
dentist Tampa	1000	$6.44
emergency dentist Tampa	140	$4.85
dentist Tampa fl	320	$4.75
pediatric dentist Tampa	110	$4.27
cosmetic dentist Tampa	73	$8.52
sedation dentist Tampa	46	$6.22
emergency dentist Tampa fl	28	$5.46
pediatric dentist Tampa fl	210	$4.29
dentist Tampa Florida	91	$6.32
best dentist Tampa	16	$8.83
walk in dentist Tampa fl	12	$5.90
cosmetic dentist Tampa fl	22	$8.74
Total	**2,068**	

A good SEO program will optimize the web pages for the above list. Did you realize that ranking for each keyword phrase has the potential of generating over 2,000 targeted visitors per month? The projected PPC costs can forecast the competitiveness of the keyword phrases. The more competitive the keyword phrases, however, the longer it can take to achieve a Page One ranking.

NOTE: As mentioned earlier, for a national campaign, your Internet marketing resource will generate a list of long-tail keyword phrases that are less competitive and easier to rank for in the short term.

Keep in mind, keyword research for a local business is different than a business who sells nationally. However, it is becoming increasingly important that a national company also incorporate a local search strategy. Trying to rank nationally for general keyword phrases can be extremely competitive and time consuming. For example, the keyword phrase "back pain relief" generates over 22,000 exact searches per month but is extremely competitive and achieving a Page one ranking would be expensive and could take over a year. When targeting a national audience, you need to discover the long tail keyword phrases that are easier to rank for. A long-tail keyword phrase is three words in length or longer and has less monthly searches, but they are easier to rank for. For example, "how to get rid of lower back pain" generates 880 exact searches per month and is less competitive. Your digital marketing consultant will use keyword research and analysis tools to determine the best keyword phrases to use for your optimization. A national campaign begins with the long-tail keyword phrases to obtain faster ranking results.

Then it expands to include the more competitive phrases to achieve good rankings in the long term. This occurs after your site grows in authority from your SEO campaign.

Our next example is also for a local business. Look at the box below for the keyword phrases and monthly traffic for a locksmith in Tampa, FL:

Keyword Phrases	Monthly Search Volume
Locksmith Tampa	1000
Tampa Locksmith	590
locksmith in Tampa	110
locksmith in Tampa Fl	46
Acme locksmith company	5
Total Traffic	**1,751**

The list represents the online locksmith market in Tampa, FL. If the Acme Locksmith Company is only ranking for its name, then it may only receive five visitors per month. If the business is also ranking Number Three for "locksmith in Tampa," the business will receive 8.5% of the 110 monthly visitors for that keyword phrase. That is about nine visitors. The total traffic Acme receives in our example is 14 visitors per month from the organic placements out of a potential of 1,751 visitors.

By not ranking for the other phrases, the Acme locksmith company is all but invisible for the majority of the surfers seeking a locksmith in Tampa, FL.

CONCLUSION

By optimizing one of their website pages for each of the keyword phrases, the Acme locksmith company could potentially rank on Page One for the entire keyword list. Additionally, by incorporating a PPC campaign to test the keyword list to determine the converting keyword phrases, the web pages can then be optimized and ranked for those phrases. Now add a Google+ Local listing, optimized video and other highly ranking content and Acme is controlling Page One with multiple placements. This is what we refer to as Niche Dominance!

It is important to remember that search engine rankings are volatile, and with increased competition, it is becoming more important that you work with professionals. Expect your rankings to fluctuate; however, if you are in a highly-specialized niche with little competition, you may not see as much variation.

If your goal is to achieve Niche Dominance, work with a professional digital marketing consulting firm with the proper experience. In subsequent chapters each topic listed above is discussed in detail, including the questions to ask vendors to ensure that you select the correct resource. The information will also assist you in managing individual resources on your own.

{ CHAPTER 6 }

Digital Order of Business #3:
Taking Ownership of your Free Online
Real Estate

Today it is expected that if you are a legitimate business, you can be found on the Internet. That doesn't mean you need an elaborate or expensive website, but rather you have proper and accurate online listings linking back to your website. In addition to the primary social media sites and Google+ Local, there are hundreds of local and niche specific directories. By taking ownership of these listings, you can receive high returns for years to come.

Unfortunately, most business owners lack not only the knowledge of where to list, but the time it takes to input and manage the data so critical to establishing a strong online foundation. If this is your situation, your digital marketing consultant can provide you with a marketing plan and assist you in implementing this strategy according to search engine best practices.

IS THERE A CATCH BEHIND THESE COMPANIES GIVING YOU FREE REAL ESTATE?

It is hard to believe that anything free will have much of an impact on your bottom line - but it does. Powerful companies like Google and Facebook are aggressively transforming their local online business listings, or Places pages, into fully functional mini websites. They are then showcased high in the search engines and given top visibility on smartphones. The reason these companies provide free online real estate is to entice businesses to eventually purchase online advertising.

You can generate customers by claiming your free online real estate, which includes a Google+ Local listing(s) and other local online business sites and directories. You can have an individual listing for each physical business location as long as you have different addresses and local phone numbers for each one.

NOTE: In addition to Google+ Local (the most powerful), the Bing and Yahoo business listings and the online business directories, you need to create Google+, Facebook, Twitter, LinkedIn and YouTube accounts specifically for your business. Posting content and videos regularly on these accounts will help with your company branding, search engine rankings and targeted traffic generation.

CLAIMING YOUR LISTINGS

A large percentage of listings have outdated or incorrect information, e.g., old numbers, false addresses, inaccurate categories, and even may be out of business. By requiring businesses to claim and optimize their free listing, it ensures that the information will be updated and accurate, thus improving the surfers' experience. If poor information is returned, then surfers may choose to use a different search engine or directory. Take advantage of the free listings Google, Bing and Yahoo offer, as well as the major directories such as Yelp and SuperPages. This can generate targeted traffic that can lead to increasing your revenue.

CONSISTENT INFORMATION REQUIRED FOR LOCAL BUSINESS LISTINGS

The entities above will need information about your business. Please refer to the checklist in Appendix A to help you compile this information.

Each local online business listing has unique fields they require for verification. It is imperative that you take ownership of the email address and password used to create these accounts. If not, you run the risk of losing the accounts if you sever your relationship with the online marketing resource. It is similar to your domain discussed earlier.

By consistently filling out this information across every business listing online, you are informing the search engines and potential customers that you are an active business. You are rewarded for this immensely as you grow your online presence. There are two primary benefits: the first is better search engine ranking for your website because of all the back links from these directory listings, and the second is the additional traffic that your website receives from people searching these directories for a business like yours.

Google has expanded the amount of real estate it gives to the Places and Maps listings in local search results. If you want to achieve a Page One ranking for Google's local search results, be sure that your information is accurate and that your listing is 100% compliant. This includes adding images, videos, ongoing testimonials and citations. A citation is a mention of your business online, which includes adding your information to the business directories, as well as blog posts and niche forums. Continuing to regularly add testimonials and citations will help provide your business with a competitive advantage and a potential Page One search engine ranking.

NOTE: It is critical that your business information is identical for each listing. Inconsistent information can hurt your search engine rankings. Also, ensure that you obtain at least ten Google+ Local reviews, as your listing will receive more credibility which will draw more attention to your listing.

REVIEWS, RATINGS AND MENTIONS ABOUT YOUR BUSINESS

Google additionally searches the different business listing sites, e.g., TripAdvisor, Manta, Merchant Circle, Local.com, etc. to provide searchers with better insights. This includes pricing information, reviews, photos and anything they can pull into your Google+ Local page for you. To compliment this, you should continue to gather and post reviews for your business from your happy and satisfied customers. You should also quickly respond to those customers who have written you a poor review; this is called reputation management.

Getting your company reviews posted on Google+ Local will also improve your business' chances of ranking well. Some businesses have hundreds of reviews on Google. If you really want to obtain new customers, work to achieve several hundred positive reviews on Google and other business directories. The best practice is to put a system in place to gain them slowly and consistently over time. Additionally, ask that the customer weave the keyword phrase that you wish to rank for into the testimonial along with other helpful information about their experience doing business with you.

Here are some simple strategies for soliciting reviews from your customers:

- Call and ask your best customers for a review.

- Append the request to e-mail newsletters.

- Ask for a review during customer follow-up calls.

- Study the results of a satisfaction survey and e-mail a review request to happy customers.

- Install a review station in your place of business where customers can leave reviews on iPads or other devices.

Gathering reviews from real customers on a consistent basis will yield great returns for your business. While reviews are critical, don't fall into the trap of paying for fake reviews. This can actually get your listings banned. It is much better to focus on engaging with your customers to obtain real testimonials.

OFFERS AND COUPONS

Your Google+ Local account will come automatically with its own dashboard that helps you track impressions and actions after proper verification.

An overlooked element of Google+ Local and local business online listings is posting special offers and coupons. Filling out an offer can drive tremendous amounts of traffic to your front door, as most consumers make a buying decision based on a good offer. Google rewards businesses that post quality offers associated with their business. They have implemented an advertising approval process to ensure the quality of the offer and match the ads to the users expressed interest.

QUESTIONS TO ASK

If you decide to hire an Internet marketing consultant to handle claiming your online real estate, be certain to ask the following questions:

1. Will you claim my Google+ Local and other listings using an email address I can access?

2. How do you make my Google+ Local listing 100% compliant?

3. To which business directories and citation sites will you submit my business?

4. Will you help me with testimonials?

5. Will you ensure you are using images that are not copyrighted or belong to other business owners?

CONCLUSION

It is imperative to claim your online real estate and have these numerous sites link back to your website. In addition to the SEO and traffic value described, it will help with your company branding.

{ CHAPTER 7 }

Digital Order of Business #4: Search Engine Marketing (PPC Advertising Campaigns)

Once you have your website updated for conversions, including your mobile ready website and your list of keyword phrases, you can begin your search engine marketing (PPC) campaign. This will generate immediate targeted traffic which can convert into sales. The goal is to test and ensure that your website content and calls to action are converting and to determine the keyword phrases that are generating the sales. The goal is to eliminate bidding on the keyword phrases that are used by shoppers and bid more on the keyword phrases that send the buyers to your site.

NOTE: Most businesses are reluctant to invest in a PPC campaign because they view it as expensive or have had a bad experience. These bad experiences usually occurred because they attempted to do it themselves or did not work with a professional. We highly recommend that you discuss this with your internet marketing consultant and incorporate a professional PPC campaign.

The primary search engine marketing or pay-per-click advertising (PPC) networks are Google AdWords, Yahoo, Bing and Ask. Additionally, you can run a PPC campaign on Facebook. Since Facebook works differently, we will cover it at the end of this section, and since Google is the largest, we will use them in our example here. With PPC advertising, you create small ads that are run either on the search engine results pages or on websites with similar content.

What is attractive about a PPC advertising model is that you are only paying for the actual traffic you receive. You are not charged when your ad displays on the search pages. You pay every time someone clicks on your ad, which is linked to your website. You bid on keyword phrases that represent your business and that people are actually searching for. The primary benefit is that the traffic is highly targeted. For example, if a surfer enters "chiropractor in Tampa" into the search engines and clicks on your ad about your chiropractic services, there is a better chance of converting the visitor into a new patient. Essentially, you are offering exactly what the surfer is looking for. Additionally, Google offers PPC mobile advertising which allows you to target potential customers on mobile devices.

MOBILE ADVERTISING

Mobile advertising works similarly to pay-per-click advertising. Your ads are displayed on mobile phones when users search Google using their cell phones. The user can call your business directly and they will be sent to your mobile-ready website or asked to download a mobile application if you provide one. With one in seven searches being conducted by mobile devices and one in three mobile searches for a local business, it is advisable to make this part of your online marketing strategy. Additionally, 50% of mobile searches lead to a purchase.

According to Google, 42% of people who see a mobile ad click on it and, "With mobile advertising, you can reach targeted audiences across platforms and devices with Google Mobile Ads. You can grow online sales, send more customers to your store, or build your brand across top websites and apps with innovative mobile ad formats."

With the competitive challenges of ranking for Internet traffic, running a mobile advertising campaign can help your business generate leads and increase returns from potential customers.

A WORD OF CAUTION

It is not advisable to use mobile advertising if your website is not mobile-ready. If cell phone users cannot navigate your regular website, they will get frustrated and leave. You will be paying for traffic that you cannot convert into business. Your online marketing resource will understand how to incorporate an effective mobile marketing strategy into your overall marketing campaign. This is discussed thoroughly in a later chapter.

THE PPC ADVERTISING OPTIONS

Search Network

The search network displays your ad at either the top of the page or as one of the eight ads on the right side of the page when searchers enter the keyword phrases (as shown on page 16). For example, if they are searching for a chiropractor in Tampa and type that into Google, the chiropractor ads will appear at the top and right side of the search results page.

If you bid too low, your ad will not appear on Page One, or may not run at all if your bid is below the minimum. This minimum is determined by Google, based in part upon how much your competitors are bidding on your keyword phrases. Bids are applied within the Google Adwords dashboard.

Your ads' placement ranking on the page depends upon both the bids and click through rate (CTR) of your ad. For instance, if your ad is receiving more clicks, it may be displayed in a higher position than another advertiser who is bidding higher but has less of a click through rate. This is Google's way of rewarding good ads that produce results.

CONTENT NETWORK

The Best Way to Lose Weight - Helpful Hints For Losing Those Extra Pounds

5 Foods you must not eat
Cut down a bit of your belly fat. Never eat these 5 foods again.
Beyonddiet.com

Sign up for Google Offers
Coming soon - Find great deals in your city from Google Offers.
www.Google.com/offers

Medifast - Official Site
Lose Up To 2-5 lbs Per Week Now! Medifast - Simple, Fast, Effective.
www.Medifast1.com

Weight Loss Tampa
Physician-Supervised Weight-Loss Diet, Lose Weight, Medical
agemanagementoptimalwellness.com

◄ ►   AdChoices ▷

The desire to lose weight is common, but finding **the best way to lose weight** can be difficult. Avoid quick fad diets that make unrealistic claims and guaranteed success. No weight loss program is effective for everyone. It's better to learn about many different weight loss techniques and choose the ones that work best for you. Try using a smaller plate to help manage your portion sizes. Research has found that people have a tendency to eat the food in front of them, regardless of the serving size. Try filling a smaller plate with smaller amounts of food, and you may be surprised at how well this works for squelching any feelings of deprivation.

One effective weight loss strategy is to replace as many of your drinks as possible with water. Juice, tea, soda and coffee are high in calories. Water is the free, zero-calorie alternative drink that makes you feel full.

High calorie foods should be a target of scrutiny when attempting to lose unwanted weight. For example, eating cake isn't a bad thing, but try to focus on making it healthy. Possibly choose to have a smaller piece of cake,

The content network displays your ad on websites that display Adsense ads. Google pays a percentage of its advertising revenue to the webmasters displaying those ads. If someone has a website offering weight loss tips, for example, the Google ads for weight loss will appear on those websites. When visitors click on the ads, they are taken to the advertiser's website. Google then pays a percentage of the money they charged you for the click to the website owner.

HOW THE PPC PROCESS WORKS

PPC advertising is a skill and involves more than just bidding on keywords. Campaigns need to be managed and ads need to be continually tested. While it is the fastest way to generate targeted traffic to your website, it is also the quickest way to lose your shirt in the shortest period of time if either you or your PPC resource has limited experience.

To run a successful PPC campaign, you need to take the following actions:

- Keyword research to determine the actual keyword phrases that people type into the search engines when they are looking for a business like yours.

- Create ads using those keyword phrases according to Google's guidelines.

- Create a landing page on your website with a strong call to action; ad traffic should be sent to a landing page and NOT your home page.

- Include tracking code to determine which keyword phrases are generating actual leads.

- Determine the geographic radius for your ads to run. For example, you do not want your ad for Tampa running in Cleveland.

- Determine your daily advertising budget.

- Regularly test different ads to measure and improve the pull or click through rate (CTR) of the ads in order to reduce ad costs.

- Test your landing page to ensure that your call to action is generating conversions.

CONVERTING TRAFFIC INTO POTENTIAL CUSTOMERS

The overall goal of a well-executed PPC campaign is to reduce your advertising costs while determining the money keyword phrases. A money keyword phrase is one that generates prospects on a regular basis. Keyword phrases that generate traffic but do not convert into customers are referred to as "tire kickers" or "shoppers." A good PPC resource will look at this information and begin to eliminate the tire kicking phrases. He or she can then use that part of your PPC budget to expand your bidding on the money keyword phrases. They will also test your landing pages to ensure that the call to action is effective. For instance, if your page is receiving PPC traffic and there are zero conversions, the landing page needs to be improved. When conversions begin, then the keyword phrases can be fairly tested. The ultimate goal is to drive down your cost-per-lead. Once you know the keyword phrases that are converting, you can stop bidding on the non-converting keyword phrases and increase your budget for the converting keyword phrases.

We have seen cases where a campaign began bidding on a few hundred or more keyword phrases. As the above process was followed, the keyword list was reduced to just three that converted into customers. Now imagine how many new customers you can obtain by spending your ad budget only on the keyword phrases that you know can convert. Now realize how much money you are wasting by continuing to bid on untested keyword phrases that generate traffic but do not convert into customers.

Hot Tip: Once you know your money keyword phrases, you can use them to further optimize your website pages and use them in your online marketing campaign. When they also rank on Page One, the free organic traffic will come from your money keyword phrases.

BUDGETING FOR YOUR PPC CAMPAIGN

Your budget will depend upon the competitiveness of your business niche. Click costs are calculated on a keyword basis and the demand for each keyword phrase. While the costs can vary, we have seen phrases that generate good traffic range from 50¢ to over $100 per click!

Many businesses begin with a monthly budget based upon the competition. The budget is divided into a daily ad spend limit which allows the budget to be spread out equally over 30 days. Without a limit, the clicks and costs can be shockingly high. If this occurs before you have determined your money keyword phrases, it can be a financially painful experience.

WHAT TO WATCH OUT FOR WHEN CHOOSING A PPC RESOURCE

What we noticed most when discussing our clients' previous PPC experiences was that most vendors will usually only send traffic to the home page. Most of the clients had no idea of how much traffic they were receiving that actually converted into customers. Vendors would show them the traffic statistics and say, "Look how we are delivering for you."

To be fair, a vendor cannot be responsible for your business, what you sell, or if people will buy it. So it is safer and easier to just send traffic to your site. With this approach, the results can be disappointing as there is no conversion tracking.

When you hire a PPC firm, they should advise you on the way a proper PPC campaign needs to be incorporated into your online marketing and advertising campaigns. Even if they do not provide you with landing page support, they ought to instruct you on how it should be done correctly. They can even recommend a web designer to create your landing pages. However, the web designer should understand the function of a landing page and be able to build it with the proper layout and call to action. What you don't want is someone who can just create a standard web page and has no idea about how a landing page functions.

PPC FEE STRUCTURES

There are a variety of ways that PPC firms charge. The following are the most common:

- Set up Fee | Fixed Monthly Charge

- Set up Fee | Monthly Management Fee

- Set up Fee | Monthly Management Fee | Percentage of Ad Spend

- Set up Fee | Mark up click cost

Set Up Fee

The set up fee is charged to create your PPC campaigns and ads within Google and the other search engines where you will be advertising. This is a one-time charge, although sometimes it is waived in order to get your business.

Fixed Monthly Charge

This is a program that charges you a fixed monthly amount and includes the PPC budget and management fees. Many vendors have you pay Google directly and invoice you separately for the management fee.

Monthly Management Fee

This is charged to monitor and manage your PPC campaigns.

Percentage of Ad Spend

In addition to the monthly management fee, many firms will charge a percentage of how much money you actually spend on your PPC campaign. This can add an additional 5 to 10% cost to your PPC budget.

Mark Up Click Cost

Rather than charge a monthly management fee, many PPC firms will mark up the cost per click. For example, if your actual click cost is 52¢, they will charge you 55¢ or so. Google has cracked down on the historic price gouging and if you select this pricing model, then make sure you work with a reputable firm that is Google certified.

As mentioned above, sometimes smaller firms will establish a PPC account for each search engine in the client's name. This allows you to directly pay Google and the others for your ad costs using your credit card. The set up and management fees are paid directly to the PPC firm.

FACEBOOK PPC ADVERTISING

You can also run a PPC advertising campaign on Facebook. However, it works differently than the keyword targeted ad campaigns that were described above. With Facebook, you determine your demographics and the ads are served based upon your requirements. You can include gender, age range, location and even topics of interest if available; Facebook then informs you of the amount of traffic available based upon your criteria. Obviously, narrowing the criteria lowers the traffic amount, so it is better targeted.

It is best to test a small campaign to see if the Facebook advertising model works for your business. You should set up a separate landing page for your Facebook ad traffic to measure the results separately from your other PPC campaigns.

IS USING PPC ADVERTISING RIGHT FOR MY BUSINESS?

The best way to determine this is to do the math. First, determine how much a new customer is worth in added revenue. Is it a one-time sale or will it produce recurring revenue? See what the average PPC cost is per click; since not everyone buys, estimate that it may take 10 clicks or more to gain a new customer. This is more easily determined once you find your money words. Professional PPC programs test daily to manage your account. The first two months of testing will provide the converting keyword phrase trends that are a good benchmark for SEO and content marketing plan.

For example, if a new customer spends $100 and it takes 10 clicks to gain a new customer at $2.50 per click, then the $100 sale costs you $25. This is a $75 gain. If the average cost per click is higher than your return then you need to discuss your alternatives with a PPC professional.

RECOMMENDATION

With all the PPC firms and payment options available, we recommend that you avoid firms charging a percentage of ad spend on top of a management fee. You should also avoid the firms that charge a fixed monthly fee that includes your ad spends. We have run the numbers and this is not a good business decision. In order for a PPC firm to be profitable using this model, they need to include bidding on less expensive, low demand keyword phrases. Furthermore, most do not roll over any remaining ad budget to the next month.

As an example, one of our attorney client's primary converting keyword phrases was $7 per click. The PPC vendor he was using at the time included bidding on phrases that had only a few clicks a month for a cost of only 5¢ per click. These phrases were not converting. At $7 per click the ad spend would not go very far since it included the management fee.

The vendor would not share how their fees were earned when we reviewed our client's account. Avoid this scenario even though it appears to be a better deal. Another suggestion is to ask for a list of the keyword phrases and Google's suggested cost-per-click. See if the math works and then ask the hard questions.

We recommend that you work with a firm that actually is Google certified. It means they understand the science, as well as the mechanics of how PPC works.

QUESTIONS TO ASK

If you wish to use a PPC vendor, then ask them the following questions:

1. Are you Google certified in PPC? If no, why not?

2. Are you experienced running Facebook ad campaigns?

3. How does Google AdWords differ from Facebook?

4. Does your firm actually run PPC campaigns or do you outsource to another vendor?

5. Do you conduct the keyword research? Will you include the estimated cost per click for the keyword phrases so I can gauge expenses?

6. Can I review and approve the keyword list?

7. How do you determine the keyword phrases that buyers use as opposed to the shoppers?

8. Do you know how to spy on my competitors PPC keywords to determine which are converting?

9. Will you continually test my PPC campaign, and how? What do you perform to help with conversions?

10. Are you planning to continually test my landing page to help increase conversions?

11. What are your fees and is a contract required? Explain.

12. If my monthly ad spend is not completed, does the balance rollover into the next month?

13. Do you require a contract? If so, for how long?

14. If your campaigns are not performing, how do I get out of the contract?

15. Will you provide a list of your current PPC clients who can be used as references?

16. What kind of monthly reports will I receive? Will you review the results with me to make sure I understand how these results impact my business?

17. All PPC firms offer traffic, so how are you different from your competition?

18. Give me three reasons why I should work with your firm.

NOTE: Google recently introduced a *set it and forget it* PPC program called Adwords Express for local businesses. You create an ad, determine whether to send traffic to your Google Maps Place page or website; and Google recommends a budget based upon the ad competition. Additionally, you can also set your own budget. Be aware, though that you are responsible for measuring the conversion rate that ensures you are running a profitable campaign.

CONCLUSION

Improperly conducting a PPC campaign can prove to be a costly mistake. Traffic without conversions is motion... not productivity. We've seen instances where businesses loved that the phone was ringing but were shocked to find out they were actually losing money. We suggest that you do your homework and have a true PPC professional advise you properly and manage your campaign according to sound PPC principles.

{ CHAPTER 8 }

Digital Order of Business #5:
Search Engine Optimization (SEO)

SEO refers to making your website attractive to the major search engines so they give your web pages "Page One" positioning. This process is also referred to as making your website "search engine friendly." It is important to remember that the search engines do not rank your website as a single entity, but rather your individual web pages are indexed and ranked independently. An SEO campaign can take months to achieve a Page One ranking, however, unlike a PPC campaign, the results can be long term. Incorporating a solid SEO campaign for your business' website is the core to achieving Niche Dominance.

There are three components for conducting an SEO campaign:

- Keyword Research, which was covered in Digital Order of Business #2.

- "On Page" SEO

- "Off Page" SEO

"ON PAGE" SEO

On Page SEO refers to how you make your web pages conform to search engine guidelines (search engine friendly). The following lists a few of the major components:

- Conduct and select the correct keyword phrases based upon your niche market.

- Write original content – at least 800 -1,000+ words per page that include the keyword phrases for each page.

- Ensure that your Meta tags and web page content is unique for each page to avoid duplicate content penalties.

- Properly interlink the pages using keyword rich anchor text.

- Provide outbound links to authority sites, such as Google News and niche specific content sites and forums.

- Add the appropriate legal pages.

- Include a site map which is a list of pages contained in your web site that helps visitors and search engine bots find your web pages.

- Use quality video on your home page to engage visitors and increase the time spent on your site.

TIP: If you are having a new site developed, make sure your On Page SEO is implemented at the beginning of the development process. This will prevent your site from having to be revamped after the web developer completes the website. This is not only more efficient, but your site will be launched correctly; no one wants to make SEO changes after a website has just been launched. Many web designers offer On Page SEO but, you need to feel confident they understand it. Many will just add some content to the Meta tags, even though this is incorrect. To ensure that they can perform the optimization correctly, ask them to provide a keyword list including exact match traffic amounts per keyword phrase for your approval.

Many of our clients paid a web designer to include On Page SEO, and we discovered that the resource used guesswork and the required SEO was incomplete. This resulted in a major SEO overhaul of the entire website.

The On Page SEO portion of the project is usually a one-time fee unless you are adding content regularly.

"OFF PAGE" SEO

Off Page SEO represents an ongoing monthly program that is designed to help your web pages build authority while ranking in the search engines. This process needs to be implemented slowly over time. If not, your site will probably fail to rank well. The primary Off Page SEO technique is adding one-way back links to your web pages. These links are from blogs, directories, Web 2.0 properties, posted articles, videos and other sites associated with your niche. Off page SEO is migrating to include "social signals" in addition to the back links. A social signal is a social media action, such as: Facebook Likes, Twitter Retweets, Google +1 or Check In. Social signals are viewed as credibility and helps to improve your website rankings. A good SEO firm will continuously monitor your site's progress. With increased online competition, you need to continue the Off Page SEO program even after you achieve a Page One ranking. Rankings are not permanent and can change if your competition is also vying for a Page One ranking.

Your SEO resource will run an initial report to determine where your web pages are ranking for each of the approved keyword phrases. That report will be used as a benchmark to measure progress. Remember, you may make good progress and then suddenly find your rankings falling off, only to regain their position again. It is important to understand that this is natural. It can take four to six months to achieve a Page One ranking for competitive keyword phrases, so it is vital to incorporate a continuous Off Page SEO program to maintain the rankings.

With SEO, no resource can promise you a Page One ranking since Google and the other search engines are responsible for determining page rankings.

Many SEO firms will say they will not charge you until they achieve a Page One ranking for one or more of your web pages. If you find this attractive and wish to test them, be sure that you negotiate an agreement up front. In addition, keep in mind that many firms will rank you for your business name or an obscure keyword phrase because that makes it easy to achieve ranking. This can be more of a marketing gimmick than a productive evaluation of their SEO services.

If you are uncertain, ask them to provide you with a recent keyword list with monthly search volume for your business, e.g. plumber Charleston, plumber in Charleston, Charleston SC plumber, etc. Review the list and select one of the keyword phrases that has good traffic. Make a deal with them that if they can rank your home page for that keyword phrase, then you will work with them. Be sure that the ranking survives beyond the "Google Dance" period, and realize that it can potentially take a few months if you are in a niche that has stiff competition. However, if they agree and deliver, then you know that you have a good SEO resource.

QUESTIONS TO ASK

If you wish to hire an SEO resource, ask them the following questions:

1. How long have you and your company been providing SEO services?

2. Does your firm have any marketing experience or are you just a technical company? Please explain.

3. May I call your customers or references?

4. Have you lost any clients, and if so, why?

5. Can you show me any of your clients current Page One ranking results?

6. Do you provide a competitive analysis of my key competitors? How do you use this information?

7. Do you perform keyword research and will you review the results with me?

8. For the keyword phrases you recommend, can you provide me with the exact search count for each and the amount of traffic my site should receive when ranking on Page One?

9. How long will it take to achieve a Page One ranking? (If they offer a ranking guarantee, do not use them)

10. Do you follow search engine SEO best practices to avoid having my website penalized by the search engines? Please explain.

11. Please explain the tasks you perform for On Page SEO. It should be more than just the Meta tags.

12. Will you be optimizing my entire site or just the home page?

13. How often will you review my web pages to help improve conversions?

14. Do you plan to make a back up of my current site in case any technical issues arise?

15. How will my web site traffic be tracked? Will you install Google Analytics?

16. Are you planning to deliver monthly SEO reports? Will they be more than just a Google Analytics printout? Please explain.

17. Are you planning to deliver monthly SEO reports for the selected keyword phrases? Will you interpret the results?

CHAPTER 9

Digital Order of Business #6: Social Media - Hype vs. Reality

Social media is quite the rage and it is important that you understand what it means to your small business. A major benefit of using social media is building a positive reputation with your customers because research shows that people put high value on peer reviews and word of mouth.

Yes, you need it - but don't expect the creation of new accounts to instantly drive customers to your door. Social media is a long term solution and requires a plan, much more so than just making regular posts to Facebook or Twitter. An entrepreneur can use social media to achieve immediate branding and skyrocket national or international sales. An example of such a company is *Silly Bandz* who focused their marketing on using social media because they lacked a marketing budget. They sell animal rubber bands that children and celebrities became obsessed with. They currently have over 1.2 million Facebook likes (http://www.facebook.com/silly-bandz). Social media helped the product to become a craze.

NOTE: Entrepreneurs tend to oversell their products instead of concentrating on building their brand. The direct sales approach can lead to disappointing results for the time invested. A better approach is to use the social media platforms for relationship building with potential customers.

However, most small and local businesses feel disappointed when they view social media as a form of immediate advertising to increase revenue.

According to both a Wall Street Journal blog and a study by a social-media advisory company called Roost.com, only 15% of the average local business's fans are in the city where the business is located.

Additionally, a new survey from the Pew Internet & American Life Foundation indicated the internet and primarily search engines are the top information sources to find local businesses. The breakdown was as follows:

RESTAURANTS, BARS & CLUBS

When it comes to finding information about bars, restaurants and clubs, 51% use the internet overall, with this breakdown:

- Search engines – 38%

- Specialty websites – 17%

- **Social media – 3%**

OTHER LOCAL BUSINESSES

When it comes to seeking information about other types of local businesses, 47% use the internet, with the breakdown this way:

- Search engines – 36%

- Specialty websites – 16%

- **Social media – 1%**

Currently, the primary benefit of social media is for branding your business and building a list of potential customers. The objective is to build social proof that you are a reputable company and want to help those that are interested in what your business offers. When visitors to your social media pages begin following you and benefit from your free information, they may then decide to buy from you.

A major value not widely communicated is how social media contributes to your search engine rankings. It is increasingly being integrated into how search results are displayed and personalized for users. Google is using social media in part as a gauge to determine if your web pages belong on Page One. It is advisable to ensure that your content marketing program be tied into your social media campaign. For example, if you post a great video on YouTube, it can then be posted on your Facebook, Twitter, Google+ and LinkedIn pages. With the posts linking back to your website, you will generate traffic and back links that help your SEO rankings. In addition, when your social media posts are optimized properly, they can rank in the search engines along with your web pages and other posted content.

It is also important to understand the culture of each social media platform. People go to Facebook for relationships, information and to have fun, while they go to LinkedIn for business only. Understanding the culture is important and you need to post accordingly.

In a recent study of over 5,000 businesses, HubSpot found that traffic from LinkedIn generated the highest visitor-to-lead conversion rate at 2.74%, almost 3 times higher than both Twitter (.69%) and Facebook (.77%). In other words, of all the traffic that came to these business' websites via social media, .98% of that traffic converted into leads, compared to LinkedIn's 2.74%. However, for restaurants and clubs, Facebook plays a major role.

When deciding which social media platform your organization should use, start first with your audience. Ask your current customers which social media sites they frequent and why; it will provide some insight about your customers to help with your marketing efforts.

The following defines the major social media platforms:

Facebook

Facebook is the Mecca of social media. It's where you can find every type of audience imaginable. Millions of people use Facebook every day to keep up with friends and family, share links and videos, learn more about the people they meet, not to mention being able to upload an unlimited number of photos. Facebook's mission is to give people the power to share and make the world more open and connected. Facebook has over one billion users. People on Facebook do not want to be sold to; they are looking to have fun and they like to see companies giving back! To see how large organizations are effectively using Facebook, check out: http://www.facebook.com/mountaindew and http://www.facebook.com/Aflac.

GooglePlus

The GooglePlus profile is an extension of your current Google account. It is similar to a Facebook profile. It makes connecting on the web more like connecting in the real world. Different people are interested in various parts of your business. Whether it's breaking news, updates, promotions, links, photos, - even talking face-to-face with groups via easy-to-use video chat, GooglePlus lets you easily share the right things with the proper customers. Currently, early GooglePlus adapters are people who are technology savvy.

NOTE: A GooglePlus Page is different than the profile. It is a web property that is provided for your business. It is similar to a Facebook Fan page. As the GooglePlus page can rank on Page One, as well as influence your website rankings, you want to make it part of your SEO campaign.

LinkedIn

LinkedIn can be viewed as an online version of a business networking group. You can make contacts that will lead to partnerships with new vendors or even use it as a prospecting tool. The same rules apply; you want to offer value to others in return for the value they can provide your business. LinkedIn is B2B (business to business), as opposed to B2C (business to consumer).

Twitter

Twitter connects businesses to customers in real-time. Businesses use Twitter to quickly share information with people interested in their products and services, gather real-time market intelligence and feedback, and build relationships with customers, partners and influential people. Twitter is a great place to brand your organization's personality and it is easy to talk directly to an individual anywhere in the world. It's also "the" place to join a conversation.

Social Media Watch

Two new photo sharing social media sites, Pinterest and Instagram, have become popular recently but their specific business value has yet to be determined. However, we suggest that you keep current on their potential to help your business.

Pinterest

Pinterest is a Virtual Pinboard that lets you organize and share all the beautiful things you find on the web. People use pinboards to plan their weddings, decorate their homes, and organize their favorite recipes. It is growing rapidly and it is worth exploring your potential customers' activities. You can do so by browsing pinboards created by other people.

Instagram

Instagram is a fast, beautiful and fun way to share your life with friends through a series of pictures. With this service, users snap a photo with their iPhone, choose a filter to transform the look and feel, and send to Facebook, Twitter or Flickr – it is easy and is referred to as photo sharing, reinvented. Instagram provides a photo sharing and editing mobile application that instantly turns mobile users into photographers. People can like and make comments about your images. Instagram has become the "go to" application and was purchased by Facebook.

YouTube

YouTube is a video-sharing website on which users can upload, view and share videos.

YouTube displays a wide variety of user-generated video content including movie clips, TV clips, and music videos, as well as amateur content such as video blogging and short original videos. Most of the content on YouTube has been uploaded by individuals, although media corporations including CBS, BBC, VEVO, and Hulu offer some of their material via the site, as part of the YouTube partnership program.

Unregistered users can watch videos, while registered users can upload an unlimited number of videos. Videos considered to contain offensive content are available only to registered users at least 18 years of age.

YouTube videos rank very quickly in the search engines and should be a component of every small or local business's marketing campaign. They can help to brand you as an authority while driving targeted traffic to your website.

QUESTIONS TO ASK A SOCIAL MEDIA VENDOR

1. What social channel or platform do you see being the most effective for my niche?

2. Will you work with us to create a social media strategy or do you just set up accounts and post content?

3. How do you measure the success of my social media campaign?

4. What can we do to assist your efforts?

5. Do you offer exclusivity in my niche and location?

6. What types of results have you garnered for other businesses?

7. What types of realistic results should I expect?

8. Will I be responsible for all content creation or is that part of your service?

9. Do you require a contract for your social media services? How long?

10. What is the exit clause if I'm not happy with your service?

CHAPTER 10

Digital Order of Business #7: Building your Authority through Content Marketing

Once your website is optimized to achieve good search engine rankings, your online real estate has been claimed, and your business is being submitted to the business directories, this is the time to begin your content marketing campaign.

Content marketing is distributing your content to online directories, Web 2.0 properties and social media sites in different formats, such as text articles, video, audio and pdf. This achieves back links to your website, as well as additional targeted traffic from those sites. The quality of content helps to brand you as an authority. As mentioned earlier, if a unique article or video is optimized for your keyword phrase(s), it can obtain a Page One ranking simultaneously with your web pages and Google+ Local listing. This is what we refer to as Niche Dominance.

VIDEOS

YouTube is only second to Google for search traffic. Video ranks very quickly in the search engines and helps attain a

Page One search engine position for your keyword phrase(s). There are about 20 major video directories where you can distribute your videos just like an article.

However, Google can easily detect if a video contains duplicate content. A video can be recompiled with different music and animation effects to avoid duplication prior to mass distribution.

There are two types of videos: professional and link bait. A professional video is created by a media company and represents your business much like a television commercial. A link bait video looks professional but is a low cost animation with a music background. A link bait video is used for SEO back linking purposes and can drive additional traffic to your website. An example of this type of video is an automated PowerPoint presentation with a music background that is saved in a video format and uploaded to YouTube.

The best practice is using a professional video on your website to connect with your visitors. This allows them to get to know you in a way that image and text alone cannot accomplish. It is important to make it customer centric, informing them how you can help them and the benefits they will receive when they select you instead of your competition. The video should conclude with a call to action which, for example, instructs them to call you for a free estimate or consultation.

You can have a link bait video created for each of your keyword phrases and distributed to the video directories. Your digital marketing consultant should optimize the video for good search engine rankings. Just uploading a video does not ensure that it will rank on Page One of either YouTube or the search engines.

ARTICLES

There are directories, such as EzineArticles.com, that allow you to post an article for free with a back link to your website. The rule is if others want to post your article on their website or blog, they must include the resource box containing your link. If you provide good content, articles can go viral and generate an amazing amount of traffic.

However, posting the same article to multiple directories diminishes the SEO value due to duplicate content penalties. A unique version of the article should be posted to each directory for maximum SEO results. You can receive traffic from individuals searching the article directory for information; if they like your content, they will click on your link and visit your site.

NOTE: Many digital marketing vendors use a technique called "spinning" to rewrite the articles to avoid duplicate content penalties. Spinning is a software program that allows an original article to be rewritten several times using synonyms; while the meaning is the same, each reads differently. However, the search engines are increasingly able to detect spun articles and apply the duplicate content penalty to the detected copies. This reduces the value of the back links. Clearly this should be discussed with your digital Marketing consultant.

PODCASTS

A podcast is an audio file in mp3 format that can be downloaded and played on an iPod or other mp3 players. Some podcast directories even support video. Podcasts are also distributed thus providing additional back links and traffic.

CONCLUSION

Because content marketing is part of a comprehensive off page SEO program, you can discuss the requirements when you interview your digital marketing resource. Please refer to the SEO Resource Questions on page 82.

The key to incorporating a content marketing program is to syndicate your well-optimized content across the Internet, helping to brand you as an authority while generating targeted traffic back to your website. Additionally, by incorporating link diversity from the various types of properties, your web pages will rank better in the search engines.

{ CHAPTER 11 }

Digital Order of Business #8:
Going and Staying Mobile is Critical
to your Success

It's no secret that mobile phones are increasing in usage and capabilities. The mobile revolution is truly upon us, both as consumers and business owners. Major brands have already begun to experience a huge ROI by engaging with consumers via mobile devices. Most importantly, the top web companies continue to inform us of this change in behavior.

According to Google (who actually describes itself as a mobile company, not a search engine):

- Mobile searches have grown 400% over the last year.

- One in three mobile searches are for a local business.

According to Facebook

- More than 350 million active users, over 1/3 of their total user base, currently access Facebook through their mobile devices.

According to Yelp

- Their mobile application accounted for approximately 40% of all searches on their platform.

Even though local businesses realize that mobile marketing can add to their bottom line, the current challenge is grasping how to start integrating mobile strategies into their business model.

It is important to understand what mobile marketing is in a broad sense. A non-profit organization and industry leader, the Mobile Marketing Association, describes mobile marketing as: "...a set of practices that enable organizations to communicate and engage with their audience in an interactive and relevant manner through any mobile device or network." In other words, mobile connects the dots across all marketing mediums by allowing businesses and people to interact with each other through their mobile phones. By developing a proactive mobile strategy you can reduce your overall costs and increase business with prospective and current customers.

BENEFITS

- Very effective for communicating with your current customers in real time. No one leaves home without a cell phone. The devices are constantly within arm's reach.

- A mobile list of buyers adds value to the worth of your business if you wish to sell it.

- A good relationship can be built by offering valuable information in addition to *mobile customer only* discounts and specials.

- Low cost distribution system versus cost to acquire a lead is attractive.

- Owners rarely turn off their cell phones or tablets, allowing you to reach them 24/7, with impulse driven campaigns.

CHALLENGES

- Consumers become frustrated with your business if you do not provide a seamless mobile experience from your current website.

- Your list must be kept current. This requires a process to ensure new customer numbers are acquired and added to the system regularly.

- There must be planning to schedule distribution of messages.

- Sending text messages to customers without opt-in permission can get your distribution account shut down if too many spam complaints are received.

- You can face legal issues if terms are severely violated.

ENSURING THAT YOUR WEBSITE IS THUMB-FRIENDLY

The following image shows the way a traditional website displays on a mobile phone compared to a thumb friendly design.

Traditional Website

Mobile Website

If your website makes it difficult for mobile users to take action, then you are losing money, and if you are already spending money advertising your business online it gets even more painful.

Imagine a potential customer searching Google with her mobile phone for a business like yours decides to visit your website. What she sees on her mobile phone is a poorly format-ted website and she cannot take action. You just lost a sale!

If you are already spending money advertising your business online and a mobile user clicks on your PPC ad, you just paid for the click and lost the sale because he experienced difficulty trying to take action on a website that is not mobile friendly.

It is important to understand the user behavior is different when using a mobile device, as opposed to a computer. Mobile users are on the go and are looking to take action, not conduct research like they would if using a home computer. Thus, a mobile-ready website requires specific information and features and must load quickly.

Many mobile users do not subscribe to unlimited data plans and mobile networks are not as fast as an Internet connection. Accordingly, a mobile-ready website should not contain the graphics and content that a regular website usually provides.

MOBILE WEBSITE DESIGN AND FUNCTIONALITY

A mobile website is structured to display properly on a mobile phone and provides call to action type of information and functionality. These include:

- Contact information

- Location of your business (Google Maps)

- Tap-to-call feature which doesn't require dialing

- Instant access to a coupon or specials

- List of services

It is important that we reinforce this point: *if you do not offer a mobile-ready website experience to your visitors, you are losing money.* Take a moment and apply the above mobile statistics to your own business. If you are investing in a PPC advertising campaign and/or an SEO campaign to rank your website on Page One and mobile users cannot take action, calculate your loss. Just adding a mobile website solution will increase your conversions if you do nothing in addition.

NOTE: This Google tool shows you how your current site looks on a smartphone, and provides a free report with personalized recommendations tailored to how your business can build a more mobile-friendly experience. Go to: http://www.howtogomo.com.

MOBILE WEBSITE ALTERNATIVES

Restructuring your Current Website

Having your current website redesigned to be mobile-ready can be expensive. If you decide to invest in this approach, ensure that the click-to-call feature and all of the functionally listed above is incorporated.

Third Party Hosted Solutions

There are third party solutions where you can design a mobile-ready website online. If you select this solution, make sure they provide you with browser detection code for your current website. This code monitors your traffic and acts like a traffic cop. Internet traffic will remain on your website and traffic from a mobile network will automatically be sent to your mobile ready website. What you want to avoid is using a button on your current website that requires a manual click to access your mobile website because mobile users may not be able to see the button and you may lose them. Be aware that you do not own this site and have no control.

Integrated Mobile Solution on your Own Domain

You can have a mobile ready blog set up in one of two ways. The first way is to have a sub-domain created on your current website and install a mobile-ready blog. For example, if your domain is www.MyWebSite.com, then your mobile site is m.MyWebSite.com. The browser detection code is installed on your website as described above.

Registering a .mobi Domain Name

You can register a .mobi domain name instead of installing the mobile website on your current site. It works the same way as described above, however, it is on a separate domain and you own it.

Both solutions work well as of the time of this writing but there are arguments for using either option. Some question spending the money on a .mobi domain. Our recommendation is to invest in the .mobi domain and use it in conjunction with your current website. There are two primary reasons:

1. It is wise to register all your major business domain names (.com, .net, .org and .mobi). This protects your business and brand. There is nothing preventing a competitor from registering one of them and using it to compete with you on Page One. Imagine building your brand to the point that people are searching for your business and your competitor is now stealing

a portion of those potential customers because he registered one of your available domain names.

2. The rapid transition from computers to mobile devices is undisputed. Current website design may eventually become obsolete and need to be replaced, but you can still use your .com domain name for a mobile-ready website. However, by building a standard WordPress-based mobile site on a .mobi domain today, you can expand this site as the technology demands to keep you current and competitive while preserving the integrity of your current .com website. The browser detection code will continue to automatically forward the traffic from your current .com site. This approach allows you to transition over time as the technology changes, rather than having to build an entirely new site in the future because your current website can no longer support your business. When you are ready to explore incorporating a mobile solution, it is best to discuss the options with your digital marketing consultant to see which one is the correct mobile solution for your business.

CONCLUSION

In addition to a mobile website, you can build customer loyalty by incorporating a mobile texting campaign, as well as offer a mobile application to your customers. This should be incorporated with building an email customer list - both are important tools for reselling to your current customers.

{ CHAPTER 12 }

Digital Order of Business #9: Using Technology to Build Customer Loyalty

It is a fact that reselling to a current customer is much easier and less costly than marketing to obtain new customers. Yet most businesses concentrate on acquiring new customers and ignore marketing to their current customer base. Taking customers for granted, even if you provide excellent service, is never a good policy. Proactively you need to make them feel special and appreciated. It is highly recommended that you develop an internal marketing campaign, via mobile text messaging and email campaigns to increase your sales to current customers.

TYPES OF MOBILE MARKETING SERVICES

Text Messaging (SMS)

SMS stands for Short Message Service, also known as text messages. This strategy has been adopted mostly by small business owners, because the majority of cell phones are capable of sending and receiving text messages. You are limited to 140 characters per message, giving you enough space to send a short message or link to a website or coupon. According to Portio Research, 6.9 SMS trillion messages were sent in 2010. SMS traffic is expected to break 8 trillion in 2011.

Here is an example of an SMS offer:

> Reply Msg: FREE Appetizer w/ entrée. Show msg to redeem. Coupon valid today only! Watch for future deals. Text&Data Rate may apply. Reply STOP 2end.

NOTE: Text messaging allows a business to build a list of mobile phone numbers which can market to subscribers. A single text message can be broadcast to the entire list of mobile phone users on a predetermined schedule. As a business owner sees demand or supply issues with inventory they can alert members of their mobile list.

Text messaging campaigns use short numbers and specific keywords that are assigned to each campaign. For example, a dentist might say in an advertisement, *text smile to 72727*. Interested mobile users would create a text message with the word smile and send it to 72727, and then receive a message back from the dentist with a discount coupon or other reply.

NOTE: As the mobile texting networks are keyword specific, no two businesses on the same network can use the same keyword phrases. For instance, if smile was not available, "smile1" or "smile now" can be used as an alternative. The rule of thumb is to keep the keywords short and easy to spell.

Multimedia Messaging Service (MMS)

MMS is short for Multimedia Messaging Service. MMS gives you the ability to send not only text, but other content such as videos or pictures directly in messages to your customers. Because consumers are becoming more familiar with sending pictures from their phones and copying links to videos they watched on YouTube, they will welcome your creativity in communicating with them in this way. Additionally, it will help you to stand out from those just sending standard SMS texts.

QUESTIONS TO ASK

If you are interested in incorporating a mobile texting campaign, the following are questions to ask your digital marketing consultant to ensure that you launch a successful ongoing campaign:

1. How much will it cost me to send a text message?

2. Do I receive a bulk message rate by establishing an ongoing budget for messages?

3. How many messages can I use to test a campaign?

4. How many different keyword campaigns can I incorporate?

5. Does my short code change from campaign to campaign?

6. Can you integrate my text campaigns into my email list?

7. Will I be charged for both incoming and outgoing messages?

8. Will I be able to make updates to my campaign and offers?

9. Am I able to export numbers if I discontinue using your service?

10. How do I manage my text messaging campaigns?

11. Can I set up campaigns in advance and then run them on autopilot?

12. How do I track the rate of return for my text messaging campaigns?

QR CODES

The QR Code is a 2D barcode pioneered by a subsidiary of the Japanese carmaker, Toyota. Japan continues to be a leader in adopting mobile technology and has inspired a revolution with QR codes.

QR or Quick Response allows smartphone users the ability to scan the code and be directed to a specific offer in the form of video, web pages, gifts and more. Thankfully, large brands have been helping consumers understand what to do when seeing the QR code. The QR Codes have been placed as decals on ads, cars, buildings, and even coffins in Japan.

Another benefit is that you are not limited to sending someone who scans your QR code to only one web page. If you create what is called a dynamic QR code, your mobile marketing resource can update your offers without having to print costly new marketing material containing fresh QR codes. Using QR Codes is free of charge and can be an effective tool when correctly implemented into your marketing strategy.

Some QR codes can add further list building opportunities and data mining capabilities, such as user location. Additionally, linking to your social media as showcased by this Facebook QR code developed by Likify, is another way to engage with customers using creative QR codes.

NOTE: The current QR code technology will soon be replaced by near field communication (NFC). According to Wikipedia, NFC is a set of standards for smartphones and similar devices to establish radio communication with each other by touching them together or bringing them into close proximity, usually no more than a few centimeters. Present and anticipated applications include contactless transactions, data exchange, and simplified setup of more complex communications such as Wi-Fi. Communication is also possible between an NFC device and an unpowered NFC chip, called a "tag." This new technology will no longer require you to manually scan QR codes to access websites, coupons, etc.

MOBILE APPLICATIONS

A mobile application is an extra feature on smartphones which enhances the user's experience. As Apple proclaimed, "There is an app for that," and the application industry has boomed ever since.

Popular app categories include games, music, news, GPS, social networking and weather. Some are offered for free while others cost the user a nominal fee to download from their chosen App Marketplace. Highly used applications such as Google Maps or Calendars can come pre-loaded, based on the type of phone purchased.

There are endless options to make your own apps; however, one should proceed with caution. For a small business, it is a potentially costly mistake to rush into developing an app that serves no purpose. Whether you hire a highly skilled developer to build or use an app-builder, you want to be prepared and do your research. First, determine what functionality and purpose it will provide. It is advisable to use a feedback survey to ask your customers what they would like to see in a mobile app prior to having it developed.

Domino's Pizza, as an example, developed an app that allows users to build an order and track its progress right to their door. This saves customers the time of having to call in their order.

You should also establish measurable goals and benchmarks to help you evaluate your ROI. Unless you are solving a major problem, you need to have realistic expectations about your mobile apps adopted usage.

NOTE: A study by Localytics found that one in four apps downloaded are tried once and then discarded. We suggest that you begin your mobile marketing campaign by first incorporating a mobile-ready website and text messaging campaign. Once you build a mobile phone list of your customers, you can send them a message which links to a survey; the survey will provide valuable feedback as to what would comprise your mobile app functionality.

TIP: Offer them a coupon for participating and have it delivered to their mobile phone when they complete the survey.

CHANGING MOBILE ENVIRONMENT

Make sure to consider the different platforms where your app will be listed. iPhone apps differ from Android apps in compatibility and guidelines for publishing. Consider that there may be ongoing maintenance with your application in this changing environment requiring your time or that of a professional. At the time of this writing, most major brands are still trying to have their apps accepted and developed across all platforms cohesively.

NOTE: Having Google Analytics installed on your current website will indicate which types of mobile devices are accessing it the most, giving you further guidance about which platform is right for your app. In an ideal world every business would have a mobile application, available on all platforms for consumers to utilize. With the initial cost for development and ongoing maintenance and upgrades make sure that the app adds value to your customers' experience and increases your ROI. Investing in a trendy mobile app may not be the best investment.

QUESTIONS TO ASK

Here are examples of questions to ask a mobile application developer:

1. Can I see samples of the apps that you've built for other businesses like mine?

2. What functionality would you suggest for a business like mine?

3. Which mobile platforms do you specialize in and why? Are other platforms available?

4. How can you assist me in my initial app design?

5. How long will it take to develop my app?

6. What are the development milestones?

7. How do you beta test my app to ensure its functioning properly?

8. Where will my app be stored and how will my customers get access to it?

9. Do I own complete rights to my app including copyright?

10. Can I have references from your other clients?

11. What are the ongoing costs to keep my mobile app updated?

NOTE: It is advisable to establish milestones for the development process and assign a payment plan according to successful completion. Two main things that can impact the project concern making constant changes or adding additional functionality on the fly. This can be a nightmare for the programmer and more expensive for you; the more the design is solidified upfront the better. Also, make certain that the development time table is realistic and a completion date is established. To keep on track, consider planning a weekly progress call to confirm the project is moving forward. Lastly, do not launch your app to your customers until it is thoroughly tested. Not only is buggy software a nightmare, but it can turn off your customers.

EMAIL MARKETING CAMPAIGNS

To compliment your mobile customer marketing campaign, you need to also build an email customer list. If you do not have a digital list of your customers' email addresses, then gathering them and setting up the email delivery system can be painful and time consuming. Even if you have a customer tracking system often email addresses are missing, not typed in correctly, or have changed.

Once you collect and clean your email list, you need to subscribe to an email distribution system such as "Constant Contact." All you need to do is upload a spreadsheet file containing your customer names and email addresses. The system then sends out an "opt in" request to the entire list which gives you permission to email them. Finally you set up an email template to broadcast offers on a regular basis.

BENEFITS

- A list of buyers adds value to worth of your business if you wish to sell it.

- This can be very effective for reselling to your current customers.

- You can generate new ongoing revenue through relationship building.

- Build good relationships by offering valuable information in addition to customer only discounts and specials.

- Place a newsletter sign up form on your website to grow your list.

- You will incorporate a low cost distribution system.

CHALLENGES

- It can be painful and time consuming to research and "clean" the email addresses.

- The lists must be kept current and requires a process to confirm new customer emails when acquired and added to the system.

- You must plan and schedule email distributions.

- Spam complaints may be received if you email too often.

- Customers are not added to the list if they do not respond to the opt-in email request.

NOTE: Even if you do everything correctly, customers can arbitrarily click the spam button instead of just unsubscribing from your list. Why? Because it's easier than scrolling down to the bottom of the email to locate and click the unsubscribe button.

We highly recommend that you implement a customer email campaign to help generate more revenue and add overall value to your business.

{ CHAPTER 13 }

Digital Order of Business #10: Reputation Marketing

It is important that you monitor what is being said about you online. Anyone can post a bad review or negative comment which may hurt your business. Whether it is a disgruntled employee, angry customer or even a competitor, it can negatively affect your reputation and your business in general.

WHAT CAN YOU DO?

First, you must be proactive. Sign up for Google Alerts. Google will email you every time a post is indexed for the specific keyword phrases that you select. You should set up an alert for your name, business name and primary keyword phrase(s) that represent your business, e.g. chiropractor Tampa. Go to: http://www.google.com/alerts to sign up.

NOTE: Google Alerts will not locate reviews posted on citation directories, such as Yelp. You need to check those sites often to ensure that you quickly deal with any negative reviews if they occur.

Make it part of your online marketing plan to have your customers post their positive testimonials to your Google+

Local listing and other directories. By building up the positive reviews, you can counter a poor one with the volume. You should also quickly post a reply to the negative review(s) if they should occur. Always be professional and indicate what action you have taken to remedy the situation.

A more difficult Reputation Marketing situation is a post on a blog or website that is ranking on Page One. This can truly hurt your business, especially if they have achieved a top ranking for your best keyword phrases. The goal is to push the negative review off Page One so it is no longer as influential. This is accomplished by simultaneously ranking highly optimized videos, press releases, articles and other content for the keyword phases associated with the negative review. You can also create a few sites with different domain names and host them on different IP addresses.

NOTE: Usually these sites rank on Page One for low competition keyword phrases, rather than obtaining their ranking through an effective SEO strategy. Thus, incorporating an effective SEO strategy is a powerful way to address the negativity. Ensure that your digital marketing consulting firm runs a report for all the keyword phrases associated with your name, business name and niche. They can then check the Page One rankings for each to determine the extent of the issue. This will also determine the scope of the project.

By implementing a Niche Dominance program, you can have a commanding Page One presence that will help with your Reputation Marketing.

{ CHAPTER 14 }

Digital Order of Business #11: Custom Publishing

Writing a book can be considered a daunting task, especially if writing is not your passion. However, being an author is still considered a major accomplishment and something unique. It will help brand you as an authority in your niche. When watching experts interviewed in the media on a topic, you often hear something like, *"We will now hear from Jane Doe on the subject. She is the author of _____."* A book will provide you with instant credibility and offer a competitive advantage. In a fiercely competitive marketplace, a book will help you rise above the competition.

WHAT DO YOU WRITE ABOUT?

The best topics to cover are what your current customers are looking for. As a business person, think of the questions that you are usually asked. Make a list of them and you have a good beginning on a book outline.

The good news is that you do not have to write "War and Peace." The book can be under 100 pages of helpful information. People do prefer content that is short and quickly gets to the point without fluff.

Keep in mind that you are not writing the book to try and make book sales. You are writing it to build your brand, communicate your expertise and differentiate yourself from the competition. However, you can promote the book on your website's "about us" page and link to Amazon where you may make sales.

While it may seem complicated, hiring resources will make it much easier. Seeing your name on a book or hearing the reaction from people when they learn you are a published author is quite a thrill.

Your digital marketing consultant can help you to market your book online with a combination of press releases, video and social media.

NOTE: Once completed, the content can be repurposed and used as online marketing material to further brand you as an authority. For example, you can post the information to your blog and link it to your social media accounts. You can also post it to Web 2.0 directories and create helpful videos for YouTube.

Once you have implemented the 11 digital orders of business, you will have a solid foundation that should be continued to maintain your search engine rankings and online authority. You can then add supplemental online advertising programs to complement the Niche Dominance program. The following chapters will discuss these alternatives.

{ CHAPTER 15 }

Optional Online Advertising

Online advertising and lead generation services are provided by third party vendors and are not part of the Niche Dominance core. If implemented effectively, they can complement your online marketing efforts. They can be viewed as advertising - if you stop the campaigns, you lose the traffic. We suggest that you build your Niche Dominance core first before investing in these types of advertising campaigns. We provide the benefits and challenges, as well as the questions to ask vendors to help you make an informed decision.

BANNER ADVERTISING

Some services offer to post a banner or text ad across a network of websites in order to generate traffic to your website. Additionally, major television stations and newspapers offer this because their websites regularly generate a significant amount of traffic. They usually will create a graphic for your business that will link to either your website or a page on their website. This page will contain information about your company and provide contact information and a link to your website. It appears on the surface to be an attractive way to advertise to thousands of potential customers.

WHAT TO CONSIDER

Banner ad campaigns usually charge for displaying the ad and not for actual traffic generation. It is the opposite of a pay-per-click campaign. The term used is CPM (Cost per Thousand). You are charged on a per view basis, e.g., a dollar amount for every thousand times your ad displays. Do not confuse the amount of displays you purchase with the amount of traffic you will receive. What matters is how many of those viewing the web pages actually click on your ad or call you.

All that these networks promise is how many times your ad will be displayed on the websites in the network. Think of it similar to a TV advertisement; they are offering you the opportunity to be seen by their website audience whether there is a return or not. The issue with this approach is that it offers general, as opposed to targeted, traffic so it is a numbers game. To illustrate the point, which would you prefer? 1) Your ad being seen be 5,000 viewers who may or may not be interested in your offer; or 2) 10 people searching for a business like yours using a related keyword phrase proactively and clicking on either your PPC ad or your website's top search engine ranking???

BANNER BLINDNESS

Another issue for consideration is banner blindness. With the proliferation of banner ads over the years, surfers may not see your banner even when it's being prominently displayed on the page they are viewing.

Even flashing banners can be ignored. This is also considered old technology and unless tested for your market, this option may not produce the desired results for your investment. You should be conservative and expect less that a 1% return, e.g, amount of traffic for the number of displays. Remember, that is just traffic and not sales. Usually people need to see an offer about seven times before they purchase if they are not proactively searching for your solution.

QUESTIONS TO ASK

Below are suggested questions to ask the vendor:

1. Do you use general websites to display my banner ad or are they grouped by niche market? The more specific the match is the better the chance of results.

2. Do you offer statistics that track the number of displays and the click through rate to my website?

3. Will you help me to create an animated banner to improve visibility?

4. Do you guarantee a minimum click through rate for the campaign? Remember, your ad display without receiving traffic = a zero return.

5. How long am I committed to running your banner ad campaigns?

6. Can I run a test campaign to see if the campaign generates any results?

It is not recommended that you use this option as part of your online marketing campaign. If you decide to try it, then negotiate a 30-day test campaign and track the results. You should have the traffic sent to a landing page and capture the email addresses so you can follow up and build a relationship with the visitors. However, the return may not be worth the investment.

ONLINE DIRECTORY AND LEAD GENERATION SITES

Online directory lead generation companies build and rank websites to obtain traffic interested in specific topics, and then sell inclusion in the directories or the leads to businesses. They are available for most businesses and if used correctly, can help to generate additional customers. If done incorrectly, the results can be disappointing.

ONLINE DIRECTORIES

Online directories can be organized like a phone directory and include every business category; or they can be targeted exclusively to a particular niche, such as lawyers, chiropractors, etc. With a general directory, people searching them will enter the type of business they are looking for plus a location. The directory then returns the businesses listed in the directory. Many include a free listing for businesses to get them to participate and then sell sponsored listings at the top of the results page. Most will have different policies for displaying offers.

The niche specific directories can offer the same free inclusion and charge for sponsored ads at the top of the page. People searching will usually type in their location if its niche specific, e.g. chiropractors or lawyers, will organize the directory by type of practice and then return results by location.

In our experience, we discovered many directories were hurt in their SEO rankings when Google updated their algorithm, code-named "Panda." This affected their traffic. To be fair, online directories are working to recover from this change and you should just confirm that you are receiving a return for your investment.

In most cases, a free listing may not return many leads but having a link to your website from the directory helps your with SEO, as well as helping with your Google+ Local ranking.

THINGS TO CONSIDER

If you decide to try a sponsored listing, you should follow these suggestions:

1. Sign up for the shortest period of time available to test your return.

2. Verify that your web designer installs Google Analytics on your website so you can track the traffic received from the directory.

3. Use a tracking phone number in the directory ad to see how many calls you receive. Some directories offer this, as well as traffic statistics.

4. At the end of the contract, review your statistics and conversions before you decide to renew.

LEAD GENERATION SITES

There are various types of lead generation sites available targeting most niches. These are typically dedicated to a specific type of business, for instance, plastic surgeons. An example is Service Magic which offers contractors leads in their specific area. There are different business models available and what you need to determine is the quality of the lead. Leads can be either qualified or not qualified.

"QUALIFIED" LEADS

A qualified lead means that the vendor has screened the lead to fit a predetermined profile and will then send the lead via email or call you directly and transfer the call. It is then up to the business to invite the potential customer in and close the business. Even if the lead does not close, the business has to pay for the lead.

"NON-QUALIFIED" LEADS

Non-qualified leads mean that as visitors to the lead generation website fill out a website form, their contact information is forwarded to the participating business. It remains up to the business to contact the lead, introduce themselves and screen the lead. The close rate is typically low for this type of lead generation system.

ROTATION SYSTEM

Most lead generation systems use a rotation system to distribute the leads. Many limit the amount of participating businesses to prove enough of a return. Others send the same lead to multiple businesses directly who must compete for the lead.

Obviously, a qualified leads program is much more expensive but the results are stronger than a non-qualified leads program. Before you consider investing in a lead generation service, you need to first determine the value of a new customer to your business. Is the customers' purchase a one-time occurrence or do they offer a long-term revenue stream? Once you run a lead generation program, you can then determine your cost-per-lead from the service to see if it's worth continuing. As there are no guarantees, testing the alternatives in the shortest period of time possible is the correct approach.

NOTE: Some lead generation companies offer a guarantee, such as a "double your money" return for participation in their program. While this sounds attractive, most will not write you a check. Rather, they will continue to run the program until you do receive the promised return. The thing to consider is that if it's not working for your business during the contract time, why will it suddenly work if the program continues?

ALTERNATIVE TO "NON-QUALIFIED" LEADS SYSTEMS

We do not recommend subscribing to non-qualified lead generation services. Instead, incorporate an effective SEO program for your website and online marketing campaign. By achieving good rankings, you will drive targeted leads to your website and can achieve a higher conversion rate.

WEBSITE LEASING OR RENTING OPTIONS

Many digital marketing firms offer the ability for you to rent or lease their niche specific website or blog. These sites are usually already ranking on Page One and what they are offering is an opportunity for you to advertise on their site. This is a form of lead generation plus you have exclusive use of the site for a monthly price. Usually they will try to sell you other services once you begin receiving new leads from the site.

With the introduction of Google+ Local, which takes a dominating portion of Page One, you need to guarantee the traffic generated by the site is worth the investment. Many Internet marketers will register an exact match domain name for a long tail keyword phrase or a phrase that returns fewer Google+ Local listings in order to rank higher on Page One. This can result in the site only ranking for a single keyword phrase that does not generate a significant amount of traffic. However, niche targeted traffic that is steady can increase your revenue if the keyword phrase converts.

QUESTIONS TO ASK

The following questions are important to ask if you consider website leasing as an option for your online marketing campaign:

1. How old is your site and how long have you been ranking on Page One?

2. What keyword phrases has the site been optimized for?

3. What is the "exact match" local monthly traffic for each keyword phrase?

4. Where is each of these keyword phrases ranking in Google? Can I see a ranking report for the site?

5. Have you tested the keyword phrase(s) for conversion? If so, please show me your conversion report.

6. What is the monthly traffic generated by your website, and for what keyword phrases? Please show me a monthly report for the last 90 days.

7. Will I receive a monthly Google Analytics report?

8. Do you provide call tracking on the site?

9. Has anyone else previously leased the site? If so, why did they discontinue their lease?

NOTE: A Page One ranking without traffic is of little value. Unless there is consistent traffic and a high Page One ranking for the keyword phrases, then you may be disappointed with the return. On the other hand, even ranking for one keyword phrase that generates consistent targeted traffic can be worth the investment.

Do not sign a long term contract. You want to test the conversions before you commit long term. Just because a keyword phrase ranks on Page One does not mean it is a buyer's keyword phrase.

ANOTHER RENTING OPTION

A different model is when an Internet marketing firm charges you several hundred dollars up front to build a lead capture site, which they own. They will inform you that there will be no billing until the website attains a Page One ranking for a keyword phrase in your niche. Then the Internet marketing firm will register a domain name, which they also own, and will want to take control of your Google+ Local listing to link to the new site.

If you decide that you no longer wish to participate, they will attempt to lease the site to one of your competitors. They usually rank for a low traffic keyword phrase or add your zip code to the beginning of the keyword phrase to achieve ranking. They must do this, especially in competitive niches, or it could take up to a year for them to achieve a Page One ranking to get paid. For a low traffic keyword phrase and new domain name, it can take from several weeks to three months to rank, depending on the keyword phrase. They usually count on the Google+ Local listing to rank, as opposed to their website.

We do not recommend this option at the time of this writing. If you decide to invest in this option, it is important to track the traffic and conversions produced by the site to see if it is worth continuing.

PURCHASING A LEASED WEBSITE

Many digital marketing companies will offer to sell you their site once it has achieved a top Page One ranking. While it is good to have an additional site that is ranking, you must realize that rankings are not permanent. If you do not continue an effective off page SEO program, and the site becomes stagnant, the site can drop off of Page One over time. To preserve your investment, we encourage you to hire a professional SEO resource to maintain and/or improve the site's ranking. The site owner will probably offer you an SEO package if you purchase the site. Also ask to review the traffic statistics prior to purchase.

EMAIL MARKETING TO OBTAIN NEW CUSTOMERS

Many vendors offer email blasts to large opt-in lists as a marketing technique. They usually charge a fee based upon to how many email addresses that you wish to send your email advertisement. The lists are usually organized by demographics and other criteria. Essentially, you provide the ad and link to a website landing page that contains details about the offer and a call to action, which is usually a phone number or web form to fill out. The web form can add new prospects to your list as well. Some vendors offer landing pages and forward the leads to the business. While emailing a target audience of thousands of people is attractive, the returns can be disappointing. One client who later hired us indicated that he had tried a large email campaign. A vendor emailed an ad to a list of 50,000 people who fit the demographics; the cost was $6000. Here are the results as recorded by the vendors email tracking system:

Emails sent - 50,000

Number opened - 28

Clicks to landing page - 6

Calls or leads generated- 0

Obviously, it was a very painful experience. Below are some of the reasons for the poor return:

Over half of the emails ended up in the spam folder, never read.

With the fear of computer viruses and identity theft, more people are deleting emails from sources that they do not recognize, so the email was never read by this group. This could account for another third of the distribution list.

People are inundated with emails and just ignore them due to feeling overwhelmed.

People just want to buy from companies that are familiar with and trust.

The vendor re-sent the email a few days later to the same list and there was no improvement in the rate of return.

In some cases, companies have had a good return from cold email campaigns. If you wish to try it, ask the vendor if they can provide a test campaign where the list is emailed in smaller numbers. This will test the subject lines and ad content to see if your changes increase the open rate. Without great email subject lines, you would not be able to give away $10 bills unless people are reading your email messages.

The standard return is estimated to be a 1/10 of 1% return on an email blast. However, that may be high since technology and the way people react to marketing techniques is changing.

GROUP BUYING DEAL SITES

Group buying sites have been quite the rage, and even the major players such as Google and Facebook are jumping on the band wagon. The most popular are Groupon and Living Social. When Groupon was only two years old, it turned down a $6 billion deal from Google. Today Groupon has close to 80 million subscribers and was named by Forbes as the fastest growing company ever. Groupon has since gone public and added new features to their business model, such as Groupon Now. Go to: http://www.groupon.com/merchants/welcome for more information.

Although each group buying site has their own business model, conceptually they work very similarly. They post offers from businesses at a predetermined discount, such as 50%. The deal is only good if a certain number of buyers purchase. The system has viral capability which allows shoppers to communicate with others to stimulate buying to reach the minimum purchases required. Groupon handles the transactions and then pays the advertising business 50% of the revenue generated.

Group buying sites are localized to customers and less expensive than traditional advertising such as television.

However, before you get excited and run off to participate, you must determine your costs to create the deal, as well as understand the buyer psychology beforehand.

It is common to offer a 50% discount and then split the revenue 50-50 with Groupon. Do the math! Take your net revenue returned and subtract your costs from that to determine your profit. For example, if a business offers a skin treatment that usually retails for $100, and sells on Groupon for $50, you will receive $25. If the product cost and labor is $25, you're not making any money, and if the cost exceeds $25, you lose money.

Even though not everyone who purchases redeems before the expiration date, you have to anticipate that they will in order to determine your profits.

Many businesses figure that the offer is a lost leader, but it provides the potential for up sells and repeat business. While this is true in a traditional business model, customers from Groupon typically want a deal on everything and may refuse to pay more for other services. Why would someone with that mentality suddenly change their mind when they redeem their purchase and pay full retail for other products?

Make certain to plan accordingly and visit the group buying deal sites to see what your competitors are offering. Look for other deals you can offer Groupon customers when they redeem their purchase. For example, *we are offering our Groupon customers an exclusive deal if you buy today!* Do the math up front and then capitalize on the deal mentality.

BENEFITS

- Your business can experience a surge in new customers.

- Plan to receive almost instantaneous payment to help with your cash flow.

- Gather reviews from customers to post online to improve sales.

- Add these new customers to your email or mobile list.

CHALLENGES

- Your business can lose money if the wrong deal is offered.

- There is the possibility that you may not be able to handle the volume.

- You could devalue your brand by offering steep discounts.

- Groupon wants a 60-day exclusive agreement so your business cannot offer a deal on other sites.

Just remember to use sound business judgment when determining your offer and evaluate your ability to deliver to the potential surge of new customers before you enter the group buying deal marketplace.

{ CHAPTER 16 }

Conclusion

There are many reputable digital marketing companies that can help you with your business, but many specialize in only one piece of the complex puzzle. It is essential that these various vendors work together according to a plan that ensures the best results. Having the various components implemented individually does not guarantee success as an overall solution. We recommend you work with an Internet marketing consulting firm who can create a customized online marketing plan for your business, providing and/or managing your online vendors to assure successful implementation. They should understand the overall process and be able to connect the dots in a cohesive manner, which is similar to working with a home builder who manages the individual subcontractors. This prevents the roof from being built before the foundation and framing is completed. The alternative is creating the online marketing plan and managing the various vendors yourself.

TIP: If cost is an issue, consider negotiating an agreement to phase in the marketing plan according to a schedule.

With the rapidly changing online environment and fiercer competition, laying a sound framework today will provide you with an ongoing competitive advantage for tomorrow. It's what we call achieving Niche Dominance.

Visit us today at http://NicheDominance.com

Niche Dominance®

1. Transform Website
2. Verify Niche Keyword Research
3. Claim Online Real Estate
4. PPC Campaign
11. Custom Publishing
5. SEO
Your Website
10. Reputation Marketing
6. Social Media
9. Building Customer Loyalty
8. Going Mobile
7. Content Marketing

Creating order out of your digital marketing chaos

If you would like more information on how the Niche Dominance approach can help your business, please contact us at 877-609-6762 or info@NicheDominance.com.

{ APPENDIX A }

Business Information Checklist

In order to begin your Niche Dominance program, you will first need to compile the following necessary information. Your digital marketing resources will need access to your business information to create or modify your online accounts.

BUSINESS DETAILS

- Company Name

- Name of Business Owner

- Types of Payments Accepted

- Primary Contact Name

- Email

- Phone Number

- Fax Number

- Address

- Hours of Operation

- Business Website

- Year Company Founded

- Brief Description of Company's Services or Products

- Industry

- Describe Business Niche Categories

- Professional Associations or Local Organizations

- Credentials and/or Certifications that relate to your Business

- Target Market and Areas Served

- If you Were Searching for your Company, What 5 Key Words Would you Use?

- What Type of Special Can you Offer Potential Customers?

- Do you Ask for Customer Referrals/Testimonials?

- Who are your Top 3 Competitors?

- Do you Have Established Accounts with Google, Bing and Yahoo?

- Pictures and Videos

- Offers and Coupons

PROVIDE LOGINS TO:

- Google Analytics

- Google+ Local (if you have a brick and mortar location)

- YouTube

- Facebook

- Twitter

- LinkedIn

- Online Directories

- Hosting Provider

- Domain Name Registrar

- Blog

Once you compile the information, keep it for future reference. Also, if you change vendors, remember it is a good practice to change the passwords for each account.

{ ABOUT THE AUTHORS }

John S. Rizzo & V. Michael Santoro

JOHN S. RIZZO

John S. Rizzo obtained his B.S in Business Administration from the College of Charleston and then spent three years as a consultant for Amazon.com's publishing group. Over the last six years, he has assisted small and local business owners with their digital marketing strategy and served in leadership positions for multiple Chamber of Commerce initiatives that impact small businesses.

He is currently a Managing Partner with Globe On-Demand, LLC, an Internet technology company that provides online technical and marketing solutions for small and local businesses.

V. MICHAEL SANTORO

V. Michael Santoro has over 10 years of skill in the digital marketing field. Prior experience includes international senior marketing positions in high tech and national marketing positions in the medical device industry.

He has a Masters Degree from Central Connecticut State University and an undergraduate from the University of New

Haven. Additionally, Mr. Santoro was an Adjunct Professor with the Computer Science Department of Western Connecticut State University.

V. Michael Santoro is also an established nonfiction author, as well as an award winning fiction author.

He is currently a Managing Partner with Globe On-Demand, LLC, an Internet technology company that provides online technical and marketing solutions for small and local businesses.

.

www.ingramcontent.com/pod-product-compliance
Lightning Source LLC
Chambersburg PA
CBHW032303210326
41520CB00047B/1188